Certification Study Companion Series

The Apress Certification Study Companion Series offers guidance and hands-on practice to support technical and business professionals who are studying for an exam in the pursuit of an industry certification. Professionals worldwide seek to achieve certifications in order to advance in a career role, reinforce knowledge in a specific discipline, or to apply for or change jobs. This series focuses on the most widely taken certification exams in a given field. It is designed to be user friendly, tracking to topics as they appear in a given exam and work alongside other certification material as professionals prepare for their exam.

More information about this series at https://link.springer.com/bookseries/17100

Microsoft Fabric Analytics Engineer Associate Certification Companion

Preparation for DP-600 Microsoft Certification

Dr. Gomathi S

Apress®

Microsoft Fabric Analytics Engineer Associate Certification Companion: Preparation for DP-600 Microsoft Certification

Dr. Gomathi S
Coimbatore, Tamil Nadu, India

ISBN-13 (pbk): 979-8-8688-1547-8 ISBN-13 (electronic): 979-8-8688-1548-5
https://doi.org/10.1007/979-8-8688-1548-5

Copyright © 2025 by Dr. Gomathi S

This work is subject to copyright. All rights are reserved by the Publisher, whether the whole or part of the material is concerned, specifically the rights of translation, reprinting, reuse of illustrations, recitation, broadcasting, reproduction on microfilms or in any other physical way, and transmission or information storage and retrieval, electronic adaptation, computer software, or by similar or dissimilar methodology now known or hereafter developed.

Trademarked names, logos, and images may appear in this book. Rather than use a trademark symbol with every occurrence of a trademarked name, logo, or image we use the names, logos, and images only in an editorial fashion and to the benefit of the trademark owner, with no intention of infringement of the trademark.

The use in this publication of trade names, trademarks, service marks, and similar terms, even if they are not identified as such, is not to be taken as an expression of opinion as to whether or not they are subject to proprietary rights.

While the advice and information in this book are believed to be true and accurate at the date of publication, neither the authors nor the editors nor the publisher can accept any legal responsibility for any errors or omissions that may be made. The publisher makes no warranty, express or implied, with respect to the material contained herein.

    Managing Director, Apress Media LLC: Welmoed Spahr
    Acquisitions Editor: Smriti Srivastava
    Development Editor: Laura Berendson
    Editorial Assistant: Jessica Vakili

Cover designed by eStudioCalamar

Distributed to the book trade worldwide by Springer Science+Business Media New York, 1 New York Plaza, New York, NY 10004. Phone 1-800-SPRINGER, fax (201) 348-4505, e-mail orders-ny @springer-sbm.com, or visit www.springeronline.com. Apress Media, LLC is a Delaware LLC and the sole member (owner) is Springer Science + Business Media Finance Inc (SSBM Finance Inc). SSBM Finance Inc is a **Delaware** corporation.

For information on translations, please e-mail booktranslations@springernature.com; for reprint, paperback, or audio rights, please e-mail bookpermissions@springernature.com.

Apress titles may be purchased in bulk for academic, corporate, or promotional use. eBook versions and licenses are also available for most titles. For more information, reference our Print and eBook Bulk Sales web page at http://www.apress.com/bulk-sales.

Any source code or other supplementary material referenced by the author in this book is available to readers on GitHub. For more detailed information, please visit https://www.apress.com/gp/services/source-code.

If disposing of this product, please recycle the paper

To my beloved mother, whose love, strength, and wisdom continue to guide me every day, even in her absence.

This book is for you.

I miss you always.

Table of Contents

About the Author xi

About the Technical Reviewer xiii

Acknowledgments xv

Introduction xvii

Chapter 1: Exam Overview 1

    Chapter Overview.. 1

        Key Highlights of the Chapter 1

    Role of a Microsoft Fabric Analytics Engineer 2

        Responsibilities 2

        Stakeholders and Collaborations 5

    Microsoft Fabric Analytics Engineer 7

    Skills Measured at a Glance... 8

        Maintain a Data Analytics Solution 8

        Prepare Data... 11

    Implement and Manage Semantic Models... 15

        1. Designing and Building Semantic Models 15

        2. Optimizing Enterprise-Scale Semantic Models 16

    Exam Topics and Weightage Breakdown 17

        1. Maintain a Data Analytics Solution (25–30%)................................... 17

        2. Prepare Data (45–50%) 18

        3. Implement and Manage Semantic Models (25–30%)...................... 19

        Tips for Preparing Based on Weightage 20

TABLE OF CONTENTS

Certification Renewal and Updates 21
    1. Certification Renewal Overview 21
    2. Certification Renewal Process 22
    3. Updates to the Certification 23
    4. Preparing for Renewal 24
    5. Staying Ahead in Your Career 25
    Chapter Summary 25
    Pro Tips for DP-600 Exam Preparation 26

Chapter 2: Introduction to Microsoft Fabric 29
    Chapter Overview 29
    Key Terms 30
    Overview of Microsoft Fabric 33
    Key Features and Benefits of Microsoft Fabric 49
    Microsoft Fabric Architecture 56
    Integrating Microsoft Fabric with Azure and Other Tools 63
    Chapter Summary 69

Chapter 3: Implement a Data Warehouse with Microsoft Fabric 73
    Chapter Overview 73
    Key Terms 74
    Setting Up a Data Warehouse in Microsoft Fabric 78
    Data Modeling Concepts in Microsoft Fabric 85
    ETL Process with Microsoft Fabric 92
    Managing Data Storage and Performance in Microsoft Fabric 107
    Chapter Summary 114

TABLE OF CONTENTS

Chapter 4: Work with Semantic Models in Microsoft Fabric 119
Chapter Overview 119
Key Terms 120
Introduction to Semantic Models 125
Designing and Creating Semantic Models 131
Optimizing Semantic Models for Performance 137
Best Practices in Model Management 143
Chapter Summary 149

Chapter 5: Administer and Govern Microsoft Fabric 151
Chapter Overview 151
Key Terms 152
User and Access Management in Microsoft Fabric 155
Data Security and Compliance in Microsoft Fabric 162
Monitoring and Performance Optimization in Microsoft Fabric 170
Governance Best Practices in Microsoft Fabric 178
Chapter Summary 185

Chapter 6: Practice Tests and Exam Strategies 187
Chapter Overview 187
Question Types Breakdown 188
Practice Test 1: Data Warehousing 193
Practice Test 2: Semantic Models and Analytics 197
Try This Question Set 202
Exam Preparation Strategies and Tips 235

Annexure A: Key Concepts and Definitions 239

Annexure B: Common Interview Questions and Answers 251

TABLE OF CONTENTS

Annexure C: Microsoft Fabric – Specific Keyboard Shortcuts..........279

Annexure D: Case Studies and Real-World Scenarios 283

Annexure E: DAX and Power Query Cheat Sheet................................297

Index..305

About the Author

Dr. Gomathi S is a Microsoft Most Valuable Professional (MVP), MCT Community Lead, and Microsoft Learn Expert specializing in Power BI, Dynamics 365 Business Central, and AI-driven analytics. As the Head of Learning and Development, she has led numerous initiatives to bridge the academia-industry gap and empower underrepresented communities, particularly rural students and educators.

With a passion for making complex technology concepts accessible, Dr. Gomathi has trained thousands of learners around the globe through boot camps, certification programs, and mentorship. She is also the creator of the Goms Tech Talks YouTube channel, which serves as a rich learning hub for professionals and students seeking real-world tech skills.

An international speaker, published author, and active contributor to the tech community, Dr. Gomathi is on a mission to foster inclusive, impactful education in the digital era. Her work continues to inspire and enable the next generation of technology leaders.

About the Technical Reviewer

Naga Santhosh Reddy Vootukuri is a Principal Software Engineering Manager at Microsoft, working within the Cloud Computing + AI (C+AI) organization. With more than 17 years of experience spanning across three countries (India, China, and the USA), Naga has developed a rich and varied technical background. His expertise lies in Cloud Computing, Artificial Intelligence, distributed systems, and microservices.

At Microsoft, Naga leads the Azure SQL Database team, focusing on optimizing SQL deployment processes to enhance the efficiency and scalability of services for millions of databases globally. He is responsible for the entire infrastructure of the Azure SQL deployment space and has been instrumental in the development of Master Data Services.

Naga has authored and published numerous research articles in peer-reviewed and indexed journals. He is a Senior Member of IEEE and contributes technical articles as a Core MVB member at DZone, engaging with millions of active readers. He also serves as an editorial board member for a highly reputed Science journal (SCI), where he reviews research articles on Cloud Computing and AI.

In addition to his professional roles, Naga is deeply involved in the tech community as a speaker, book reviewer for Apress, and contributor to platforms like DZone and the Microsoft Tech Community. He recently served as IEEE AI summit Committee chair and lightning talk chair and selected some of the best lightning talks. He also delivered AI-related

ABOUT THE TECHNICAL REVIEWER

workshops and received an AI innovator award from Washington Senator Lisa Wellman. He also served as a judge for the Agent AI hackathon, Fabric AI hackathon, and Cosmos DB AI hackathon on Devpost, which further showcased his expertise and commitment to the advancement of technology.

Acknowledgments

With profound gratitude, I honor my father, V. Srinivasan, and my unwavering pillar of strength, my husband Anantha Krishnan A. Your steadfast support has been the bedrock of my journey and the force behind every milestone.

To my twin stars, Vishanth A. and Vishwant A.—your boundless energy, laughter, and love infuse my life with light, purpose, and joy.

I am deeply thankful to my beloved in-laws, Lakshmi V. and Appadurai K., whose encouragement has been a guiding light and a reservoir of wisdom and warmth.

To Mahalakshmi and Padmanaban, your presence echoes the unconditional love and grace of my parents. You have been a gentle and reassuring presence throughout this journey.

A special note of gratitude to my dear brother, Mr. Viswanathan S., and my wonderful sisters-in-law, Gomathy S. and Anantha Kalyani A.—your unwavering belief in me, your kindness, and your quiet strength have meant the world.

To my cherished friends, Indira P. and Kirthika B., thank you for walking beside me through every high and low. Your friendship is a treasure I hold close to my heart.

To Deepa Shirley Tryphosa Chellappa and Smriti Srivastava, your expert guidance, thoughtful insights, and patient encouragement—from the seed of an idea to its final form—have been truly invaluable.

Each of you has shaped this journey in a special way. Your love, support, and belief have been the wings beneath my aspirations—and for that, I am eternally grateful.

Introduction

The world of data is evolving rapidly—and at the center of this transformation stands Microsoft Fabric, a unified data platform that brings together everything from data engineering and science to real-time analytics and business intelligence in one seamless experience. Designed for the modern data professional, Microsoft Fabric empowers organizations to unlock the full potential of their data, driving deeper insights and more informed decision-making.

Whether you're a data analyst, data engineer, business intelligence professional, or a solution architect, Microsoft Fabric provides the tools and capabilities to modernize your analytics stack and streamline your data workflows. As enterprises increasingly adopt Microsoft Fabric, the demand for certified professionals who can navigate and utilize this platform is also on the rise.

This book is your trusted companion in preparing for the DP-600: Microsoft Certified Fabric Analytics Engineer Associate certification exam. It is tailored for

- Professionals aiming to demonstrate expertise in data modeling, data transformation, data integration, and analytics solutions within Microsoft Fabric
- Individuals transitioning from Power BI, Azure Synapse, or Data Platform backgrounds and looking to master Fabric

INTRODUCTION

- Beginners seeking a structured and practical guide to build end-to-end analytics solutions in the Fabric ecosystem
- Trainers, educators, and mentors who are looking for a ready reference to support their learners or teams

Each chapter of this book breaks down complex concepts into digestible explanations, backed by hands-on examples, practice questions, and real-world use cases that reflect the exam objectives. Whether you're aiming to upskill, reskill, or simply validate your knowledge, this guide will help you walk into the exam room with confidence—and, more importantly, prepare you to make an impact in the real world.

Let's begin the journey to becoming a Microsoft Certified Fabric Analytics Engineer Associate—one chapter at a time.

CHAPTER 1

Exam Overview

Chapter Overview

This chapter provides an in-depth overview of the DP-600 certification, focusing on the role, responsibilities, and skills required of a Microsoft Fabric Analytics Engineer. By exploring the exam topics and weightage, candidates will understand the key areas to focus on while preparing. The chapter also discusses the certification renewal process, ensuring long-term relevance in the ever-evolving field of data analytics.

Key Highlights of the Chapter

- **Role of a Microsoft Fabric Analytics Engineer**: Understanding the core responsibilities and the collaborative nature of this role within an organization.
- **Skills Measured**: A breakdown of the critical areas of expertise assessed in the DP-600 certification.
- **Exam Topics and Weightage**: A detailed analysis of the exam syllabus, highlighting the percentage emphasis on each skill area.

- **Certification Renewal and Updates**: Guidance on maintaining certification validity through periodic renewals and staying up-to-date with Microsoft Fabric advancements.

This chapter sets the foundation for the rest of the book, helping readers orient their preparation strategy and aligning their learning goals with the exam requirements.

Role of a Microsoft Fabric Analytics Engineer

A Microsoft Fabric Analytics Engineer plays a critical role in modern data-driven organizations by designing, creating, and managing analytical assets to support business intelligence and decision-making processes. These professionals bridge the gap between raw data and actionable insights by leveraging tools and technologies within Microsoft Fabric, including semantic models, data warehouses, and lakehouses.

Responsibilities

The responsibilities of a Microsoft Fabric Analytics Engineer encompass the entire life cycle of data analytics solutions which are shown in Table 1-1, ensuring that the organization can derive maximum value from its data assets.

CHAPTER 1   EXAM OVERVIEW

Responsibilities Overview

Table 1-1. Responsibilities

Responsibility	Description
Preparing and Enriching Data for Analysis	Establishing data pipelines, transforming data, and ensuring schema designs like star schemas for efficient querying.
Securing and Maintaining Analytics Assets	Implementing security and governance practices, applying sensitivity labels, and managing analytical assets for reusability.
Implementing and Managing Semantic Models	Designing and optimizing semantic models using Data Analysis Expressions (DAX), configuring relationships, and managing deployment life cycles.
Querying and Analyzing Data	Using SQL (Structured Query Language), KQL (Kusto Query Language), and DAX (Data Analysis Expressions) for advanced data analysis, creating interactive dashboards and visualizing KPIs.

These responsibilities include

1. **Preparing and Enriching Data for Analysis**

    o   Establishing data pipelines to ingest raw data into storage solutions like lakehouses and warehouses

    o   Transforming data to ensure it is clean, accurate, and aligned with analytical requirements

    o   Addressing data quality issues, including duplicates, missing values, and inconsistent formats

3

CHAPTER 1   EXAM OVERVIEW

2. **Securing and Maintaining Analytics Assets**
    - Implementing security and governance practices, such as access controls at workspace, item, row, column, and object levels
    - Applying sensitivity labels to ensure compliance with data privacy regulations
    - Managing and endorsing analytical assets to promote trust and reusability across teams

3. **Implementing and Managing Semantic Models**
    - Designing semantic models that provide an intuitive layer for data analysis and reporting
    - Configuring relationships and calculations using Data Analysis Expressions (DAX)
    - Optimizing performance for large-scale semantic models, including implementing incremental refresh strategies and Direct Lake configurations
    - Managing the deployment life cycle of semantic models through XMLA endpoints and deployment pipelines

4. **Querying and Analyzing Data**
    - Using SQL, Kusto Query Language (KQL), and DAX to perform advanced data analysis and generate insights
    - Creating dynamic, interactive dashboards and reports to visualize data and track key performance indicators (KPIs)

CHAPTER 1　EXAM OVERVIEW

Stakeholders and Collaborations

Microsoft Fabric Analytics Engineers operate at the intersection of technology and business, making collaboration with diverse stakeholders essential for success, as shown in Table 1-2.

Stakeholders and Collaborations Overview

Table 1-2. *Understanding Stakeholders and Collaborators*

Stakeholder	Collaboration
Business Stakeholders	Collaborate with executives and analysts to align analytical solutions with business goals and objectives.
Data Architects	Work with architects to design scalable data platforms and choose appropriate storage and processing solutions.
Data Engineers	Partner with data engineers to implement efficient data pipelines and transformations.
Data Analysts	Support analysts by providing enriched datasets and self-service analytical tools.
IT Administrators	Coordinate with administrators to implement security policies and ensure compliance standards are met.

Key partnerships include

1. **Business Stakeholders**

    o   Collaborate with executives, product managers, and business analysts to understand organizational goals and translate them into data requirements.

    o   Ensure analytical solutions align with strategic objectives and drive value for decision-makers.

2. **Data Architects**
   - Partner with architects to design scalable and robust data platforms that align with organizational standards and best practices.
   - Collaborate on selecting the appropriate data storage and processing solutions, such as lakehouses or warehouses.

3. **Data Engineers**
   - Work closely with data engineers to implement efficient data pipelines and transformations that meet the organization's analytical needs.
   - Ensure that data is correctly integrated and optimized for downstream use in reporting and semantic models.

4. **Data Analysts**
   - Support analysts by providing clean, enriched datasets and self-service analytical tools like Power BI and semantic models.
   - Collaborate on creating advanced calculations and reports that align with business needs.

5. **IT Administrators**
   - Coordinate with administrators to implement security policies and monitor system performance and health.
   - Ensure adherence to compliance and governance standards for data handling and storage.

Microsoft Fabric Analytics Engineers play a pivotal role in empowering organizations to make data-informed decisions by integrating technical expertise with business acumen. Their work ensures that stakeholders have timely access to reliable insights while maintaining the security and integrity of analytics assets.

Microsoft Fabric Analytics Engineer

Table 1-3. *Role-Based Responsibilities in Microsoft Fabric Analytics*

Role/ Responsibility	Business Stakeholders	Data Architects	Data Engineers	Data Analysts	IT Administrators
Preparing and Enriching Data for Analysis	✓	✓	✓	✗	✗
Securing and Maintaining Analytics Assets	✓	✓	✗	✓	✓
Implementing and Managing Semantic Models	✓	✓	✗	✓	✓
Querying and Analyzing Data	✓	✗	✓	✓	✗

CHAPTER 1   EXAM OVERVIEW

Skills Measured at a Glance
Maintain a Data Analytics Solution

The "Maintain a Data Analytics Solution" skill domain constitutes a significant portion of the DP-600 certification, focusing on the essential capabilities required to manage and optimize analytics solutions within Microsoft Fabric. This skill area emphasizes the application of governance, security, and life cycle management practices to ensure that analytical assets are reliable, secure, and aligned with organizational goals.

1. Implementing Security and Governance

Security and governance are foundational elements of maintaining a robust analytics environment. Microsoft Fabric provides various tools and capabilities to help professionals secure their data and analytics solutions effectively.

- **Workspace-Level Access Controls**
    - Define access permissions for workspaces to ensure that only authorized users can view or modify content.
    - Assign roles, such as Admin, Member, or Viewer, to manage access based on responsibilities.
- **Item-Level Access Controls**
    - Restrict access to specific items within a workspace, such as datasets, reports, or dashboards.
    - Ensure that sensitive data is only accessible to individuals who require it for their role.

- **Row-Level, Column-Level, Object-Level, and File-Level Access Control**
  - Implement row-level security (RLS) to restrict data visibility based on user roles or attributes.
  - Configure column-level security to hide sensitive columns from specific users or groups.
  - Apply object-level and file-level security to control access to specific items or files within the solution.
- **Sensitivity Labels**
  - Use sensitivity labels to classify and protect data assets based on their confidentiality.
  - Ensure that labels align with organizational data governance policies and compliance requirements.
- **Item Endorsement**
  - Endorse datasets and reports to highlight trusted assets for broader organizational use.
  - Establish a culture of data trust and encourage users to rely on endorsed assets.

2. Maintaining the Analytics Development Life Cycle

Managing the development life cycle of analytics solutions is a critical skill for ensuring that changes and updates are implemented smoothly without disrupting operations.

CHAPTER 1   EXAM OVERVIEW

- **Configuring Version Control for a Workspace**
    - Set up version control systems to track changes to data models, reports, and other analytics assets.
    - Enable collaboration among team members by maintaining a single source of truth for assets.
- **Creating and Managing Power BI Desktop Projects (.pbip)**
    - Develop and manage projects in Power BI Desktop using the .pbip format to streamline collaboration and maintain version history.
    - Share projects with team members to promote consistent development practices.
- **Deployment Pipelines**
    - Create and configure deployment pipelines to automate the migration of analytics solutions across development, test, and production environments.
    - Monitor pipeline progress and troubleshoot issues to ensure smooth transitions.
- **Performing Impact Analysis of Downstream Dependencies**
    - Analyze the impact of changes to lakehouses, data warehouses, dataflows, and semantic models on downstream reports and dashboards.
    - Ensure that updates do not break dependencies or disrupt critical business processes.

CHAPTER 1 EXAM OVERVIEW

- **Deploying and Managing Semantic Models Using XMLA Endpoint**
    - Leverage XMLA endpoints to deploy, update, and manage enterprise-scale semantic models.
    - Enable fine-grained control over model deployments and maintain consistency across environments.
- **Creating and Updating Reusable Assets**
    - Develop reusable Power BI assets, such as templates (.pbit), data source files (.pbids), and shared semantic models.
    - Promote reusability to reduce duplication of effort and enhance collaboration.

The "Maintain a Data Analytics Solution" skill domain is essential for ensuring the security, reliability, and scalability of analytics solutions in Microsoft Fabric. Mastery of these concepts enables professionals to deliver high-quality, trusted insights that empower organizations to make data-driven decisions confidently.

Prepare Data

Data preparation is a vital skill for Microsoft Fabric Analytics Engineers, as it forms the foundation for building reliable and insightful analytics solutions. This domain emphasizes acquiring, cleaning, transforming, and optimizing data to ensure it meets the requirements for analytical workflows.

CHAPTER 1   EXAM OVERVIEW

1. Getting Data

Microsoft Fabric enables users to connect to and discover data from various sources to create rich analytical solutions.

- **Creating Data Connections**
    - Establish connections to internal and external data sources, including databases, APIs, and file systems.
    - Use Microsoft Fabric tools like OneLake and Real-Time Hub to simplify data integration.
- **Discovering Data Using OneLake Data Hub and Real-Time Hub**
    - Leverage OneLake Data Hub to locate and integrate structured and unstructured data assets.
    - Utilize Real-Time Hub for streaming data ingestion and real-time analytics.
- **Ingesting or Accessing Data as Needed**
    - Choose appropriate ingestion methods for batch or streaming data.
    - Access data directly or replicate it to lakehouses, warehouses, or eventhouses.
- **Choosing Between Lakehouse, Warehouse, or Eventhouse**
    - Understand the use cases for different data storage options:
        - **Lakehouse**: For large-scale, unstructured, or semi-structured data.

CHAPTER 1   EXAM OVERVIEW

- **Warehouse**: For structured data and fast SQL-based querying.
- **Eventhouse**: For event-driven or real-time analytics scenarios.

- **Implementing OneLake Integration**
  - Enable seamless data sharing and accessibility by integrating eventhouses and semantic models with OneLake.

2. Data Transformation Techniques

Transforming raw data into a usable format is critical for generating meaningful insights.

- **Creating Views, Functions, and Stored Procedures**
  - Use SQL to create reusable views and stored procedures for data transformation and querying.

- **Enriching Data**
  - Add new columns or tables to datasets for enhanced analytical capabilities.
  - Implement calculated fields or derived metrics to meet specific business needs.

- **Implementing a Star Schema for Lakehouses or Warehouses**
  - Design and optimize star schemas to improve performance and simplify reporting.

CHAPTER 1   EXAM OVERVIEW

- **Denormalizing and Aggregating Data**
    - Flatten complex relationships and aggregate data for efficient querying.
    - Use denormalized datasets for faster analytical workflows.
- **Handling Data Quality Issues**
    - Identify and resolve duplicates, missing data, or null values.
    - Apply data profiling techniques to maintain consistency and integrity.
- **Filtering and Converting Data**
    - Use filters to extract subsets of data relevant to specific analyses.
    - Convert data types to ensure compatibility with analytical models.

3. Querying and Analyzing Data

Extracting insights from prepared data involves querying and analytical techniques.

- **Using the Visual Query Editor**
    - Utilize drag-and-drop interfaces for creating and running queries.
- **Writing SQL Queries**
    - Perform advanced querying, filtering, and aggregation using SQL.

- **Leveraging Kusto Query Language (KQL)**
    - Analyze streaming or log data with KQL's rich set of operators.

Implement and Manage Semantic Models

Semantic models simplify complex datasets by creating an intuitive layer that enables analysts and decision-makers to access and interpret data efficiently. This domain focuses on designing, building, and optimizing semantic models for scalable analytics.

1. Designing and Building Semantic Models

- **Choosing a Storage Mode**
    - Select storage modes (Import, DirectQuery, or Direct Lake) based on performance, scalability, and data freshness requirements.
- **Implementing a Star Schema**
    - Optimize semantic models by adhering to star schema principles for relationships and data hierarchies.
- **Configuring Relationships**
    - Establish relationships, such as bridge tables and many-to-many connections, to link datasets effectively.

CHAPTER 1   EXAM OVERVIEW

- **Writing Calculations Using DAX**
    - Use DAX (Data Analysis Expressions) to create calculated columns, measures, and tables.
    - Implement advanced DAX functions for dynamic calculations, filtering, and aggregations.
- **Creating Composite Models**
    - Combine data from multiple sources into a unified model to meet diverse analytical needs.
- **Implementing Calculation Groups and Field Parameters**
    - Simplify complex calculations using calculation groups.
    - Enable dynamic report customization with field parameters.
- **Large Semantic Model Storage**
    - Identify use cases for large models and configure them to handle enterprise-scale requirements.

2. Optimizing Enterprise-Scale Semantic Models

- **Improving Query and Report Visual Performance**
    - Optimize queries and visuals to reduce rendering time and enhance user experience.
    - Use techniques like pre-aggregations and query folding for efficiency.

CHAPTER 1   EXAM OVERVIEW

- **Enhancing DAX Performance**
  - Write optimized DAX expressions using variables, summarization functions, and reduced cardinality.
- **Configuring Direct Lake**
  - Set up Direct Lake for seamless querying of lakehouse data without requiring intermediate storage.
  - Configure fallback options and refresh behaviors to handle disruptions.
- **Implementing Incremental Refresh**
  - Optimize refresh operations by updating only changed or new data, reducing processing time and resource usage.

Exam Topics and Weightage Breakdown

The DP-600 certification exam assesses candidates across three primary domains, reflecting the core competencies required of a Microsoft Fabric Analytics Engineer. Each domain is assigned a specific weightage, indicating its relative importance in the exam. Understanding the distribution helps candidates prioritize their study efforts and allocate time effectively to maximize their performance.

1. Maintain a Data Analytics Solution (25–30%)

This domain evaluates your ability to secure, govern, and manage the life cycle of data analytics solutions within Microsoft Fabric. Key focus areas include

17

CHAPTER 1   EXAM OVERVIEW

- **Implementing Security and Governance**
  - Apply workspace, item, and row-level access controls.
  - Implement sensitivity labels and endorse items to ensure compliance and data trust.
- **Maintaining the Analytics Development Life Cycle**
  - Configure version control for analytics assets.
  - Manage deployment pipelines for smooth migration across environments.
  - Analyze downstream dependencies to mitigate risks during updates or changes.
- **Managing Semantic Models Using XMLA Endpoints**
  - Deploy and manage large-scale semantic models to support enterprise reporting.

This section is essential for ensuring that analytics solutions remain secure, scalable, and aligned with organizational needs.

2. Prepare Data (45–50%)

As the largest domain, this area focuses on acquiring, transforming, and preparing data for analysis. It underscores the technical skills required to build a reliable foundation for analytics workflows.

- **Getting Data**
  - Create connections to various data sources, including OneLake and Real-Time Hub.
  - Select appropriate storage solutions (lakehouse, warehouse, or eventhouse) based on use cases.

- **Transforming Data**
  - Enrich datasets with new columns or tables and design efficient schemas (e.g., star schema).
  - Address data quality issues like duplicates, null values, and inconsistent formats.
  - Perform advanced transformations, including denormalization, aggregation, and joins.
- **Querying and Analyzing Data**
  - Use SQL, KQL, and the Visual Query Editor to extract insights from prepared datasets.

Given its high weightage, this domain requires a strong understanding of data engineering principles, ensuring that datasets are clean, accurate, and optimized for analysis.

3. Implement and Manage Semantic Models (25–30%)

This domain focuses on building, deploying, and optimizing semantic models that form the analytical backbone for business intelligence solutions.

- **Designing and Building Semantic Models**
  - Choose the appropriate storage mode (Import, DirectQuery, Direct Lake) for specific scenarios.
  - Implement relationships, such as many-to-many and bridge tables, to ensure data consistency.

CHAPTER 1   EXAM OVERVIEW

- o   Write advanced DAX calculations for dynamic metrics and analyses.
- o   Develop composite models that integrate data from multiple sources.
- **Optimizing Semantic Models**
  - o   Enhance query and visual performance through pre-aggregations and optimized DAX expressions.
  - o   Configure Direct Lake and implement incremental refresh for scalability and efficiency.

This section tests your ability to create high-performing, intuitive data models that empower end users to explore and visualize data seamlessly.

Weightage Summary

Exam Domain	Weightage
Maintain a Data Analytics Solution	25–30%
Prepare Data	45–50%
Implement and Manage Semantic Models	25–30%

Tips for Preparing Based on Weightage

1. **Focus Heavily on Data Preparation**
   - o   Allocate significant time to mastering data ingestion, transformation, and querying techniques, as this domain carries the highest weightage.

2. **Master Governance and Life Cycle Management**

    o Understand security principles, deployment pipelines, and life cycle management to excel in the "Maintain a Data Analytics Solution" domain.

3. **Develop Semantic Model Expertise**

    o Practice designing and optimizing semantic models with real-world datasets to gain confidence in this critical area.

By aligning your preparation strategy with the exam weightage, you can build a solid foundation in the skills required to excel as a Microsoft Fabric Analytics Engineer.

Certification Renewal and Updates

The DP-600 certification, which validates expertise as a Microsoft Fabric Analytics Engineer, is a valuable credential that reflects proficiency in managing data analytics solutions using Microsoft Fabric. However, maintaining this certification requires periodic renewal to ensure that certified professionals stay current with evolving technologies and best practices.

1. Certification Renewal Overview

Microsoft certifications, including the DP-600, have a **renewal cycle of 12 months.** Renewal ensures that certified professionals remain up-to-date with the latest features, enhancements, and changes within the Microsoft Fabric ecosystem.

CHAPTER 1   EXAM OVERVIEW

- **Why Renewal Is Important**
    - Keeps your skills relevant as Microsoft continuously updates its products
    - Demonstrates a commitment to professional growth and staying aligned with industry standards
    - Ensures employers and clients trust your ability to handle current and future challenges
- **Renewal Eligibility**
    - You must hold an active DP-600 certification to qualify for renewal.
    - Renewal is available starting 6 months before your certification's expiration date.

2. Certification Renewal Process

The renewal process for the DP-600 certification is straightforward and designed to validate your knowledge of the latest updates without requiring you to retake the full certification exam.

- **Free Online Renewal Assessment**
    1. Microsoft offers a free online assessment for certification renewal.
    2. The assessment focuses on new features, updates, and best practices introduced in Microsoft Fabric since you originally earned your certification.
- **Key Features of the Renewal Assessment**
    1. Can be completed online at your convenience.
    2. Open book: You can refer to resources during the assessment.

CHAPTER 1   EXAM OVERVIEW

3. No additional cost: Renewal is free of charge as long as you complete it within the eligibility window.

- **Steps to Renew Certification**

    1. Visit the **Microsoft Learn Certification Dashboard**.

    2. Check for renewal notifications and access the renewal assessment.

    3. Complete the assessment within the specified timeframe.

    4. Upon passing, your certification is extended for another 12 months.

3. Updates to the Certification

The DP-600 certification aligns with Microsoft Fabric's latest features and capabilities. To reflect changes in the platform, Microsoft periodically updates the exam content and renewal assessments.

- **Frequency of Updates**

    ○ Exam content is reviewed and updated annually or more frequently if there are significant product updates.

    ○ The latest update for DP-600 was on **November 15, 2024**, ensuring coverage of new tools, functionalities, and best practices.

- **What's New in the Latest Update?**

    ○ Enhanced focus on **Direct Lake** integration and advanced **real-time analytics** scenarios.

- Updates to security topics, including **row-level, column-level, and file-level access controls**.
- Expanded coverage of **Kusto Query Language (KQL)** for querying streaming data and logs.

4. Preparing for Renewal

To successfully renew your certification, it's essential to stay engaged with Microsoft Fabric's developments and maintain your skills through continuous learning.

- **Resources for Renewal Preparation**
  - **Microsoft Learn**: Use free learning paths to explore updated features and scenarios. (https://learn.microsoft.com/en-us/training/courses/dp-600t00)
  - **Documentation**: Refer to Microsoft Fabric's official documentation for in-depth technical insights.
  - **Community Engagement**: Participate in forums, webinars, and events to learn from peers and Microsoft experts.
- **Tips for Success**
  - Regularly practice new tools and functionalities introduced in Microsoft Fabric.
  - Review your previous notes and projects to reinforce foundational knowledge.
  - Leverage the renewal assessment's open-book format to refer to trusted resources.

5. Staying Ahead in Your Career

Renewing your certification not only keeps your credentials valid but also enhances your career prospects:

- Positions you as a skilled professional who is proactive about keeping up with technological advancements.

- Ensures that your skills remain aligned with organizational and industry needs.

- Provides opportunities to explore and implement the latest innovations in data analytics.

Certification renewal is a crucial part of maintaining your status as a Microsoft Fabric Analytics Engineer. By keeping your certification current and staying informed about platform updates, you ensure that your skills remain relevant and valuable in the rapidly evolving field of data analytics. The straightforward renewal process and abundant resources make it easy to stay on top of your game and continue to excel in your role.

Chapter Summary

This chapter provides a comprehensive introduction to the DP-600 certification exam, detailing its objectives, structure, and significance for aspiring Microsoft Fabric Analytics Engineers. It highlights the critical role of these professionals in designing, managing, and optimizing analytical assets like semantic models, data warehouses, and lakehouses.

The chapter begins by explaining the key responsibilities of a Microsoft Fabric Analytics Engineer, emphasizing their collaboration with stakeholders, architects, analysts, and administrators to deliver business-driven analytics solutions. It underscores the necessity of technical expertise in tools such as SQL, Kusto Query Language (KQL), and Data Analysis Expressions (DAX).

CHAPTER 1   EXAM OVERVIEW

A detailed breakdown of the **skills measured** in the exam provides insights into the three core domains:

1. **Maintaining a Data Analytics Solution**: Focuses on securing and managing analytics assets while ensuring life cycle governance

2. **Preparing Data**: Emphasizes data acquisition, transformation, and preparation, which is foundational for analytics

3. **Implementing and Managing Semantic Models**: Highlights building, optimizing, and scaling semantic models to support business intelligence

The chapter also discusses the **exam topics and weightage breakdown**, enabling candidates to allocate their preparation time effectively. The section on **certification renewal and updates** guides readers on maintaining their certification through annual renewal assessments and staying current with Microsoft Fabric's evolving features.

Pro Tips for DP-600 Exam Preparation

1. **Prioritize Data Preparation**
    - With 45–50% weightage, mastering data ingestion, transformation, and cleaning is critical. Focus on OneLake integration and star schema design.

2. **Master Security and Governance**
    - Practice implementing row-level, column-level, and file-level security controls. Learn how to configure sensitivity labels and deployment pipelines.

3. **Strengthen Querying Skills**
   - Sharpen your SQL, KQL, and DAX skills with hands-on projects. Use sample datasets to simulate real-world scenarios.

4. **Leverage Hands-On Labs**
   - Use Microsoft Fabric environments to practice building lakehouses, warehouses, and semantic models. Experiment with Direct Lake and incremental refresh.

5. **Use Official Study Resources**
   - Follow Microsoft Learn modules and official documentation to cover exam topics comprehensively.

6. **Optimize Time Management for the Exam**
   - Practice mock exams under timed conditions to get comfortable answering questions within the 100-minute limit.

7. **Stay Updated with New Features**
   - Regularly check for updates to Microsoft Fabric since exam content is updated annually.

8. **Join the Microsoft Community**
   - Engage in forums, webinars, and study groups to gain tips and insights from experienced professionals.

9. **Focus on Weighted Areas**
    o   Spend more time on heavily weighted domains like "Prepare Data" (45–50%) while ensuring proficiency in the others.

Pro Tip Balance your preparation between theoretical knowledge and practical experience. The more you practice real-world scenarios, the better you'll perform on the exam.

CHAPTER 2

Introduction to Microsoft Fabric

Chapter Overview

This chapter serves as a foundational introduction to Microsoft Fabric, a powerful, end-to-end analytics solution that unifies data engineering, data science, real-time analytics, and business intelligence under a single SaaS offering. Microsoft Fabric is built on top of Azure and integrates seamlessly with various Microsoft services, offering a streamlined experience for data professionals.

The chapter will begin by exploring the **evolution of data analytics** and the need for a comprehensive, integrated solution like Microsoft Fabric. Readers will learn how Fabric consolidates multiple services—such as Azure Synapse Analytics, Power BI, and Azure Data Factory—into a unified platform.

Next, we will dive into the **key features and benefits** of Microsoft Fabric. This section will cover its ability to handle structured and unstructured data, support for AI and machine learning workloads, and how it simplifies data governance through Purview-powered security and compliance.

To further understand how Microsoft Fabric works, the **architecture** section will break down its essential components. This includes discussions on the **OneLake storage system, Data Factory, Synapse Data**

CHAPTER 2   INTRODUCTION TO MICROSOFT FABRIC

Engineering, Synapse Data Science, Synapse Real-Time Analytics, and Power BI. By understanding these elements, readers will see how Fabric enables data professionals to build, transform, and analyze data seamlessly.

Lastly, the chapter will cover **integration with Azure and other tools**, explaining how Microsoft Fabric interacts with Azure Data Services, Microsoft 365, third-party applications, and external data sources. Readers will see how Fabric can be integrated into their existing data ecosystem to enhance scalability, governance, and efficiency.

By the end of this chapter, readers will

- Understand what Microsoft Fabric is and why it is important.
- Recognize the key components and benefits of Microsoft Fabric.
- Gain insights into the architecture and how different services interact.
- Learn how Microsoft Fabric integrates with Azure and other Microsoft tools.

This chapter will lay the groundwork for the rest of the book, ensuring that readers have a strong foundation before diving deeper into Fabric's features, best practices, and certification-focused insights.

Key Terms

Microsoft Fabric Core Concepts

- **Microsoft Fabric:** A unified analytics platform integrating data engineering, data science, and business intelligence.
- **OneLake:** The central data lake in Microsoft Fabric that provides a unified storage layer.

CHAPTER 2   INTRODUCTION TO MICROSOFT FABRIC

- **Lakehouse**: A hybrid data architecture combining the benefits of a **data lake** and a **data warehouse**.

- **Data Warehouse**: A structured storage system optimized for SQL-based analytics.

- **Data Pipeline**: A workflow that moves and transforms data across Fabric services.

- **Real-Time Analytics**: The ability to process and analyze streaming data instantly.

Data Processing and Storage

- **Structured Data**: Organized data in a defined schema, such as tables in SQL databases.

- **Unstructured Data**: Raw data that does not follow a predefined structure, such as images, videos, and logs.

- **ETL (Extract, Transform, Load)**: A data integration process that extracts data, transforms it, and loads it into a target system.

- **ELT (Extract, Load, Transform)**: A variation of ETL where data is loaded first and then transformed as needed.

- **Kusto Query Language (KQL)**: A language used for querying real-time analytics data in Fabric.

Integration and Connectivity

- **Azure Data Factory**: A cloud-based ETL service used to integrate and transform data.

- **Azure Synapse Analytics**: A powerful analytics service for big data and data warehousing.

- **Power BI**: A business intelligence tool for interactive data visualization.
- **Microsoft Purview**: A data governance solution that provides security and compliance controls.
- **Hybrid Data Integration**: Connecting on-premises and cloud data sources for seamless analytics.
- **Data Gateway**: A bridge that allows secure data transfer between on-premises data and Microsoft Fabric.

Security and Governance

- **Role-Based Access Control (RBAC)**: A security model that controls access based on user roles.
- **Data Lineage**: The ability to track the flow and transformation of data over time.
- **Compliance and Regulations**: Ensuring data privacy and security standards, such as **GDPR, HIPAA, and SOC 2**.

Performance and Scalability

- **Serverless Computing**: A cloud-based execution model where resources scale automatically.
- **Auto-Scaling**: The ability to increase or decrease computing power based on demand.
- **Multi-Cloud Compatibility**: The capability to integrate with multiple cloud platforms (Azure, AWS, Google Cloud).

CHAPTER 2   INTRODUCTION TO MICROSOFT FABRIC

Overview of Microsoft Fabric

1. **Introduction to Microsoft Fabric**

    Microsoft Fabric is a unified analytics platform designed to integrate data engineering, data science, real-time analytics, and business intelligence into a single, seamless experience. It brings together the capabilities of multiple Microsoft data solutions—including Azure Synapse Analytics, Power BI, and Azure Data Factory—into a fully managed, AI-powered SaaS solution.

    This platform is built to address the increasing complexity of data management by providing a **centralized** and **scalable** approach to handling large datasets, ensuring security, and simplifying analytics workflows.

    1.1. **Why Microsoft Fabric?**

        Modern businesses generate vast amounts of data from multiple sources, requiring robust data storage, processing, and analytics solutions. Traditionally, organizations have relied on multiple tools, leading to fragmented workflows, data silos, and increased operational overhead.

        Microsoft Fabric was developed to resolve these challenges by offering:

        An all-in-one analytics platform: Eliminates the need for separate services for data integration, transformation, and visualization.

Seamless integration with Microsoft products: Works smoothly with Azure, Microsoft 365, Power BI, and other Microsoft tools.

Scalability and performance: Supports massive datasets, real-time processing, and AI-driven insights.

Governance and security: Built-in data governance using **Microsoft Purview** ensures compliance and data protection.

By unifying the data ecosystem, Microsoft Fabric empowers data professionals—from engineers to analysts—to collaborate more efficiently. The platform introduces a new concept called **OneLake**, a single, unified data lake that serves as the foundation for all data storage and access within Fabric. This shared data layer reduces redundancy, improves discoverability, and enables users to build end-to-end data workflows without constantly moving or duplicating data. Moreover, with features like **Direct Lake mode**, data can be queried instantly in Power BI without the need for traditional import or refresh operations, significantly improving performance and reducing latency. Microsoft Fabric also supports open data formats and APIs, enabling interoperability with existing systems and ensuring future-proof analytics investments.

2. **Core Capabilities of Microsoft Fabric**

Microsoft Fabric provides a **unified** and **comprehensive** approach to data analytics through its various services and capabilities. Below are the

CHAPTER 2   INTRODUCTION TO MICROSOFT FABRIC

key components that form the foundation of the platform:

2.1. **OneLake: The Unified Storage System**

OneLake is Microsoft Fabric's **centralized** data storage solution, designed to eliminate data silos and provide a **single source of truth** for all analytics workloads. It offers:

- **Auto-discovery of data** from various sources (Azure, AWS, on-premises, etc.)
- **Delta Lake compatibility**, enabling structured and unstructured data processing
- **Fine-grained security and governance** using Microsoft Purview

Example

Imagine a retail enterprise with data spread across multiple systems: customer purchase data in Azure SQL Database, inventory data in AWS S3, and store operations data hosted on on-premises SQL Server. Traditionally, integrating this data would require building complex pipelines, moving data across environments, and managing multiple storage layers.

With **OneLake**, all these data sources can be virtually unified within a single, centralized lake. The Azure SQL and on-premises SQL data can be ingested into OneLake using **Dataflows Gen2** or **Data Factory pipelines**, while the AWS S3 data can be accessed using shortcuts or data virtualization capabilities. Once inside OneLake,

35

this data becomes discoverable and queryable by different personas—like data engineers, data scientists, and business analysts—without duplicating or physically moving data.

For example, a Power BI report can directly connect to customer and inventory data stored in OneLake using **Direct Lake mode**, allowing fast, real-time analytics with minimal refresh overhead. Simultaneously, Microsoft Purview ensures data access policies are consistently enforced across all data layers, maintaining security and compliance.

2.2. **Data Engineering with Synapse**

Fabric integrates **Synapse Data Engineering**, allowing organizations to perform **big data processing** and **data transformation** at scale. Key features include:

- **Apache Spark-powered** processing for scalable ETL operations
- **Low-code/no-code data transformation** using Dataflows and Pipelines
- **Integration with SQL and Python-based data processing tools**

Example

A healthcare provider needs to consolidate patient records, insurance claims, and wearable device data into a centralized analytics system. Using **Synapse Data Engineering in Microsoft Fabric**, a data engineer creates a Spark notebook

CHAPTER 2   INTRODUCTION TO MICROSOFT FABRIC

that processes terabytes of semi-structured JSON data from wearable devices, applies transformations to clean the data, and merges it with structured patient records from SQL databases.

For less technical tasks, the same team uses **low-code Dataflows Gen2** to apply standard transformations like column renaming, data filtering, and aggregations. The team also leverages Python within Synapse notebooks to run advanced calculations on patients' vital statistics and output the cleaned datasets directly into **OneLake**, where they're ready for reporting or machine learning.

2.3. Data Factory for ETL and Orchestration

Microsoft Fabric includes a revamped **Data Factory**, which enables

- **ETL (Extract, Transform, Load) pipelines** to connect to on-premises and cloud-based data sources
- **Built-in connectors** for databases, SaaS applications, and cloud services
- **Integration with Azure Data Factory** for existing workflows

Example

A logistics company collects delivery tracking data from multiple regional systems. Using the **revamped Data Factory in Fabric**, they design an ETL pipeline that extracts data from on-premises

Oracle databases, applies transformations to standardize timestamps and addresses, and loads it into a centralized OneLake Delta Table.

They utilize built-in connectors to pull traffic data from Google Maps API and combine it with delivery data to optimize delivery routes. The entire workflow is orchestrated using scheduled triggers, and for legacy pipelines, they easily integrate with their existing **Azure Data Factory** workflows through linked services.

2.4. Data Science and AI Capabilities

Fabric provides AI-powered insights through **Synapse Data Science**, which allows users to

- Develop **machine learning models** using Azure Machine Learning.
- Perform **predictive analytics** with built-in ML libraries.
- Use **AutoML** for no-code AI-based forecasting.

Example

An e-commerce company wants to predict customer churn. A data scientist uses **Synapse Data Science in Fabric** to build a machine learning model. They begin with **Azure ML integration**, pulling customer behavioral data from OneLake. After exploratory analysis using built-in ML libraries like `scikit-learn`, they train a classification model that predicts churn likelihood.

CHAPTER 2   INTRODUCTION TO MICROSOFT FABRIC

For non-technical business users, the team enables **AutoML**, allowing them to generate predictive models by simply selecting a dataset and target variable. This democratizes AI, enabling marketers to forecast campaign effectiveness or sales managers to anticipate revenue trends—without writing code.

2.5. Real-Time Analytics with Synapse

For businesses requiring **real-time** data processing, Microsoft Fabric offers **Synapse Real-Time Analytics**, enabling

- **Streaming data ingestion** from IoT devices, social media, and APIs

- **Event-driven analytics** for detecting patterns and trends instantly

- **Integration with Apache Kafka and Event Hubs** for real-time dataflows

Example

A smart city project monitors real-time traffic data from thousands of IoT sensors across roads and intersections. These sensors stream data—such as vehicle count, speed, and weather conditions—into **Synapse Real-Time Analytics** via **Event Hubs**.

The system ingests this data in real time, applies event-based triggers to detect traffic congestion or accidents, and alerts city traffic management through Power BI dashboards. By integrating with **Apache Kafka**, they also feed the real-time

39

CHAPTER 2   INTRODUCTION TO MICROSOFT FABRIC

stream into historical trend analysis, enabling predictive maintenance of traffic signals and road infrastructure.

2.6. Power BI for Visualization and Reporting

Power BI is embedded within Microsoft Fabric, allowing users to

- Create **interactive reports and dashboards**.
- Perform **ad hoc analysis** on large datasets.
- Use **Copilot AI-driven insights** to uncover hidden patterns in data.

Example

A multinational retail chain uses **Power BI embedded in Microsoft Fabric** to monitor sales performance across all global branches. The sales data—ingested into OneLake—is visualized using **interactive dashboards** that display KPIs like revenue, product performance, and regional trends.

Analysts perform **ad hoc queries** on large datasets using Direct Lake mode, without waiting for dataset refreshes. They also use **Power BI Copilot** to type natural language queries like "Show me the top 5 selling products in Asia last quarter," and instantly get AI-generated visuals and summaries, boosting data-driven decision-making across the organization.

Table 2-1. *Core Capabilities of Microsoft Fabric with Use Cases*

Core Capability	Description	Key Benefits	Use Case/Scenario
OneLake (Unified Data Lake)	A centralized, **single storage layer** for all data workloads in Fabric.	Eliminates data silos, enables seamless data sharing across Fabric services.	**Retail Chain Analytics:** A global retailer centralizes sales, inventory, and customer data in OneLake to enable cross-regional reporting and insights.
Lakehouse Architecture	Combines the **best of data lakes and data warehouses** in a single solution.	Supports both **structured and unstructured data**, optimized for analytics.	**Financial Services Risk Analysis:** A bank uses the lakehouse to analyze structured transaction records and unstructured customer feedback for risk management.
Data Integration and ETL	Uses **Data Factory, Dataflows, and Pipelines** to ingest, transform, and orchestrate data.	Simplifies data movement across services, supports **low-code/no-code ETL**.	**Healthcare Data Processing:** A hospital system integrates patient records from multiple clinics for a unified **electronic health records (EHR) system**.

(continued)

Table 2-1. (*continued*)

Core Capability	Description	Key Benefits	Use Case/Scenario
Data Warehousing	A **fully managed, scalable warehouse** optimized for SQL-based analytics.	Supports **T-SQL compatibility, direct Power BI integration, and AI-powered optimizations**.	**E-Commerce Customer Insights:** An online store leverages data warehousing to track customer purchases and generate personalized recommendations.
Real-Time Analytics	Processes **streaming and event-driven data** using **Kusto Query Language (KQL)**.	Enables **real-time monitoring, anomaly detection, and predictive analytics**.	**Manufacturing IoT Monitoring:** A factory uses real-time analytics to process sensor data and predict machine failures before they occur.
AI and Machine Learning Integration	Uses **Synapse ML, Azure Machine Learning, and Copilot AI** for intelligent analytics.	Enhances decision-making with **AI-driven insights and predictive modeling**.	**Fraud Detection in Banking:** A bank deploys AI-powered models to detect suspicious transactions and prevent fraud in real time.
Power BI Native Integration	Built-in **Power BI** for **interactive dashboards, reports, and self-service analytics**.	**No need for separate BI tools**, seamless visualization with Fabric data sources.	**Supply Chain Optimization:** A logistics company builds **Power BI dashboards** for real-time shipment tracking and performance analysis.

(*continued*)

Table 2-1. (*continued*)

Core Capability	Description	Key Benefits	Use Case/Scenario
Security and Governance	Powered by **Microsoft Purview, Azure AD, and RBAC** for compliance and security.	Ensures **data privacy, governance, and role-based access control (RBAC)**.	**Pharmaceutical Compliance Reporting:** A drug manufacturer secures patient trial data and ensures compliance with **HIPAA and GDPR** regulations.
Multi-Cloud and Hybrid Support	Connects with **Azure, AWS, Google Cloud, and on-premises data sources**.	Provides **flexibility in data storage, processing, and analytics** across platforms.	**Telecom Customer Data Management:** A telecom company integrates call data from AWS, Google Cloud, and on-premises systems to provide a **unified customer experience**.
Serverless and Auto-Scaling	On-demand **compute and storage scaling** for optimized performance.	Reduces **operational costs** and **improves workload efficiency**.	**Streaming Video Analytics:** A media company processes large volumes of user engagement data dynamically without **manual infrastructure management**.

3. **How Microsoft Fabric Unifies the Data Life Cycle**

   Microsoft Fabric is **not just a collection of tools** but a **fully integrated** platform that connects all stages of the data life cycle:

   1. **Data Ingestion**: Using **Data Factory**, organizations can extract and integrate data from multiple sources.

   2. **Data Storage**: OneLake provides a single, secure repository for structured and unstructured data.

   3. **Data Processing**: Data Engineers can leverage **Synapse Data Engineering** for ETL and transformation.

   4. **AI and Analytics**: Data Scientists can build ML models with **Synapse Data Science**.

   5. **Real-Time Insights**: Businesses can monitor live data using **Synapse Real-Time Analytics**.

   6. **Business Intelligence**: Power BI enables stakeholders to create dashboards and reports for decision-making.

   Unified Experience Through Deep Integration

   a. **All Workloads Under One Roof**

      Microsoft Fabric consolidates multiple analytics capabilities—data engineering, data integration, data science, real-time analytics, and BI—into a **single SaaS environment**. This means:

      - No need to switch between Azure Synapse, Data Factory, or Power BI as separate services.
      - Everything runs on a **shared compute engine** (based on Spark) and is connected to the same storage layer (OneLake).

CHAPTER 2   INTRODUCTION TO MICROSOFT FABRIC

b. **OneLake: The Common Storage Backbone**

All components—whether it's a Synapse notebook, a Data Factory pipeline, or a Power BI report—read/write data to **OneLake**, the unified data lake.

- This eliminates data duplication.

- Enables **Direct Lake access** for blazing-fast analytics.

- Makes data discoverable across tools without manual integration.

c. **Interoperable Workflows**

You can build an end-to-end pipeline like this:

- Use **Data Factory pipelines** to bring in data from Salesforce or SAP.

- Clean and transform data using **Synapse Spark notebooks** or **low-code Dataflows**.

- Use **Synapse Data Science** to train ML models on the processed data.

- Perform **real-time monitoring** via **Synapse Real-Time Analytics** from IoT feeds or webhooks.

- Visualize everything using **Power BI**—all within the same interface.

Each of these workloads talks to each other **natively** through Fabric, avoiding third-party connectors or extra service setups.

45

d. **AI-Powered Insights Across the Stack**

- Copilot is embedded throughout Fabric—helping in **Power BI** for insights, **Synapse Notebooks** for code generation, and **Data Factory** for pipeline suggestions.

- AutoML is integrated into **Data Science** experiences, making it easy for business users to experiment with AI.

e. **Centralized Governance with Microsoft Purview**

Security and compliance policies apply uniformly, thanks to tight integration with **Microsoft Purview**:

- Row-level and column-level security can be applied across Synapse, Power BI, and OneLake.

- You can monitor lineage from ingestion to visualization.

Real-World Benefit: A Single Pane of Glass

In traditional analytics setups:

- A data engineer works in Synapse.

- A data scientist logs into Azure ML.

- A BI analyst opens Power BI separately.

- Data moves multiple times, causing version control issues and latency.

With Microsoft Fabric, all these users log into the **same portal**, use the same storage, and build on each other's work **without friction**.

CHAPTER 2 INTRODUCTION TO MICROSOFT FABRIC

4. **Microsoft Fabric vs. Traditional Data Analytics Platforms**

   To understand the value of Microsoft Fabric, let's compare it with traditional data analytics solutions in the following table:

Feature	Microsoft Fabric	Traditional Platforms
Unified Platform	Yes—combines multiple analytics tools in one.	No—requires separate services.
Storage	OneLake (centralized, scalable, secure).	Multiple data lakes and warehouses.
Integration	Native integration with Azure, Power BI, ML.	Requires third-party connectors.
Governance and Security	Built-in compliance with Purview.	External governance solutions needed.
AI and Automation	Copilot-powered insights and AutoML.	Limited AI capabilities.
Scalability	Designed for big data workloads.	Performance varies by service.

5. **Business Use Cases for Microsoft Fabric**

   Organizations across industries can leverage Microsoft Fabric for various analytics needs. Some common use cases include

   5.1. **Retail and E-Commerce**

   - **Customer insights** using AI-powered analytics
   - **Real-time inventory tracking** with streaming data

- **Personalized recommendations** using ML models

5.2. **Healthcare and Life Sciences**

- **Predictive diagnostics** using AI and real-time analytics
- **Secure patient data management** with OneLake
- **Data integration from multiple sources** (hospitals, research labs, etc.)

5.3. **Financial Services**

- **Fraud detection** using AI-driven analytics
- **Risk assessment** with real-time market data
- **Automated compliance monitoring** using Purview

5.4. **Manufacturing and IoT**

- **Industrial automation** using streaming IoT data
- **Predictive maintenance** for equipment failures
- **Supply chain optimization** with Power BI dashboards

Key Features and Benefits of Microsoft Fabric

1. **Introduction**

   Microsoft Fabric is designed as an end-to-end, AI-powered, and highly integrated analytics platform that brings together multiple data services under one unified solution. Unlike traditional data platforms that require multiple tools for storage, data engineering, real-time analytics, and visualization, Fabric simplifies the analytics journey by combining these functionalities into a single, scalable, and secure environment.

   This section will explore the **key features** that make Microsoft Fabric a game-changer for data professionals, along with the **benefits** that organizations can leverage to improve their analytics capabilities.

2. **Key Features of Microsoft Fabric**

   Microsoft Fabric introduces a wide range of features that enable seamless data integration, governance, AI-driven insights, and real-time analytics. Below are its core capabilities:

   2.1. **Unified Data and Analytics Platform**
   - Fabric integrates **data engineering, data science, real-time analytics, and business intelligence** into a single platform.

- It eliminates the need for **separate tools** such as Azure Synapse, Power BI, and Azure Data Factory by combining them into a single solution.
- Users can **seamlessly transition** between different workloads without switching between multiple services.

2.2. **OneLake: The Centralized Data Storage**

- **OneLake** acts as a **unified storage system** across all Fabric workloads, ensuring that all data is stored in a single, scalable, and structured format.
- It is **built on Delta Lake**, offering ACID compliance, version control, and schema enforcement.
- Data can be **shared and reused** across different teams without duplication.
- **Shortcuts feature** allows businesses to **connect external storage locations** (AWS S3, Azure Data Lake, etc.) directly within Fabric.

2.3. **AI-Powered Insights and Copilot**

- **Copilot in Fabric** allows users to generate **AI-driven insights**, create reports, and transform data using **natural language**.

CHAPTER 2   INTRODUCTION TO MICROSOFT FABRIC

- AI-powered automation enables
    - **Auto-generated dashboards** in Power BI.
    - **AI-assisted data preparation** for ETL processes.
    - **Predictive analytics** for business intelligence.
- Supports **Azure Machine Learning** and **AutoML** for training models directly within Fabric.

2.4. **Synapse-Powered Data Engineering and Science**

- Microsoft Fabric incorporates **Synapse Data Engineering** and **Synapse Data Science**, allowing
    - **Large-scale data transformations** using Apache Spark.
    - **Advanced data modeling** with SQL, Python, and R.
    - **Seamless integration with Jupyter Notebooks** for AI/ML workloads.

2.5. **Real-Time Data Processing with Synapse Real-Time Analytics**

- **Streaming analytics** supports ingestion from IoT devices, event hubs, and social media platforms.

51

CHAPTER 2 INTRODUCTION TO MICROSOFT FABRIC

- Enables **real-time anomaly detection**, fraud prevention, and time-sensitive decision-making.
- Supports **low-latency analytics** on massive datasets using **Kusto Query Language (KQL)**.

2.6. Power BI Integration for Business Intelligence

- **Power BI is natively embedded** within Microsoft Fabric, offering
    - **Self-service BI capabilities** with drag-and-drop visuals
    - **Auto-refreshing dashboards** connected to real-time data sources
    - **AI-powered insights** using natural language queries
- Users can build reports directly from **OneLake without moving data**.

2.7. No-Code/Low-Code Data Integration with Data Factory

- Microsoft Fabric includes a **revamped Data Factory**, providing
    - **Over 200 pre-built connectors** to integrate with SQL Server, Salesforce, SAP, and more
    - **Visual drag-and-drop pipeline creation** for ETL workflows
    - **Integration with Azure Data Factory**, ensuring migration is seamless

2.8. Built-In Security, Compliance, and Governance with Microsoft Purview

- Fabric is **natively integrated with Microsoft Purview**, enabling
    - **Unified data governance** across the entire data life cycle
    - **Access control and data lineage tracking** for compliance
    - **Sensitivity labeling** to prevent unauthorized data exposure
- Supports **role-based access control (RBAC)** and **multi-factor authentication (MFA)** for security

2.9. Serverless and Scalable Architecture

- **Fabric is fully managed (PaaS/SaaS), eliminating infrastructure concerns.**
- Scales automatically based on workload demand, ensuring cost efficiency.
- **Consumption-based pricing model** allows businesses to pay only for what they use.

3. Key Benefits of Microsoft Fabric

3.1. Simplicity and Ease of Use

- **All-in-one platform** eliminates the need for managing multiple tools.
- **User-friendly interface** with low-code/no-code features for nontechnical users.

- **Copilot AI** allows natural language queries, making analytics more accessible.

3.2. Cost Efficiency

- Reduces **infrastructure costs** by replacing multiple services with a single SaaS solution.
- **Auto-scaling** prevents over-provisioning and unnecessary spending.
- Pay-as-you-go model ensures businesses only pay for actual usage.

3.3. Improved Collaboration and Productivity

- **OneLake enables a unified data repository**, allowing different teams (data engineers, analysts, and business users) to work on the same dataset without duplication.

  Seamless integration with **Microsoft 365 (Excel, Teams, SharePoint)** for easy data sharing.

- Power BI's **real-time dashboards** improve decision-making.

3.4. AI-Powered Insights for Better Decision-Making

- **Copilot AI** automates report generation, forecasting, and data transformations.
- **AutoML** simplifies machine learning model creation.
- **Built-in predictive analytics** helps businesses anticipate trends.

3.5. Scalability and Performance

- **Handles petabyte-scale datasets** with serverless architecture
- **Supports structured and unstructured data** (JSON, CSV, Parquet, etc.)
- **Optimized query performance** using Delta Lake and Synapse engines

3.6. Strong Data Governance and Security

- **Microsoft Purview integration** ensures compliance with GDPR, HIPAA, and SOC 2.
- **Data lineage tracking** helps maintain audit trails.
- **Enterprise-grade security features** like encryption and role-based access control.

3.7. Seamless Integration with Azure and Third-Party Tools

- Works natively with **Azure services** like Synapse, Data Lake, Machine Learning, and Event Hubs.
- **Supports hybrid and multi-cloud environments**, including AWS and Google Cloud.
- **Pre-built connectors** allow integration with third-party tools like Snowflake, Salesforce, and SAP.

CHAPTER 2   INTRODUCTION TO MICROSOFT FABRIC

Microsoft Fabric Architecture

1. **Introduction**

   Microsoft Fabric is a **unified, AI-powered data analytics platform** designed to bring together multiple data services into a single, cohesive solution. It integrates data engineering, real-time analytics, data science, and business intelligence while maintaining a **scalable, secure, and cost-effective architecture**.

   The architecture of Microsoft Fabric is built on **a lake-centric approach (OneLake)**, where all data is centrally stored and shared across different workloads. It also leverages **Synapse-powered analytics**, **Power BI integration**, and **AI-driven automation** to create a seamless experience for data professionals.

   This chapter provides an in-depth breakdown of *Microsoft Fabric's architecture*, explaining how its components work together (Figure 2-1).

CHAPTER 2   INTRODUCTION TO MICROSOFT FABRIC

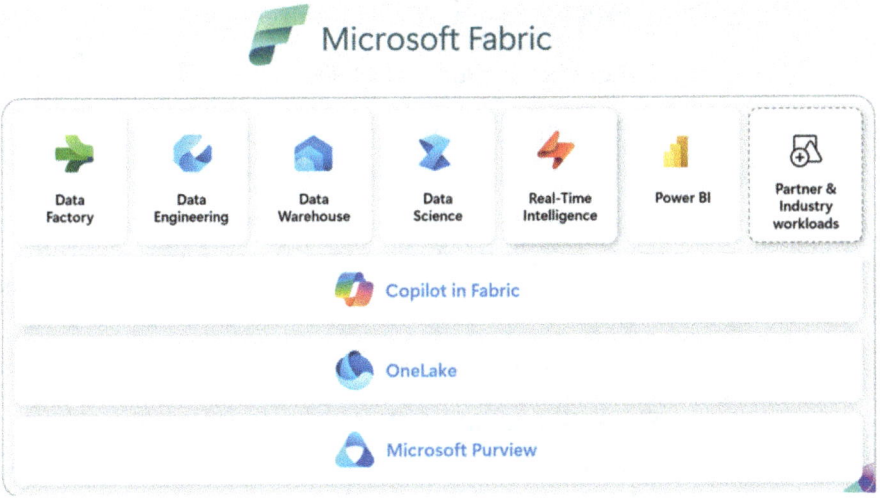

Figure 2-1. *Microsoft Fabric architecture and its components. Source: Microsoft Fabric documentation*

2. **Core Components of Microsoft Fabric Architecture**

   Microsoft Fabric consists of the following key architectural components:

   1. OneLake (Unified Data Lake)

   2. Synapse-Powered Analytical Workloads

   3. Data Integration Layer (Data Factory and Pipelines)

   4. Real-Time Analytics (Event Streams and KQL Databases)

   5. Business Intelligence with Power BI

   6. Security, Compliance, and Governance (Microsoft Purview Integration)

   7. Copilot AI and Automation

   8. Scalability and Performance Optimization

3. **Deep Dive into Microsoft Fabric Architecture**

    3.1. **OneLake: The Unified Data Lake**

    OneLake is the foundation of Microsoft Fabric, providing **a single, unified storage layer** that connects all workloads. It follows a **lakehouse architecture**, combining the best of data lakes and data warehouses.

    Key Features of OneLake:

    - **Single Source of Truth**: All Fabric workloads share the same data repository.
    - **Delta Lake-Based Storage**: Ensures **ACID transactions, versioning, and schema enforcement**.
    - **Built-in Data Governance**: Integrated with **Microsoft Purview** for **access control, data lineage tracking, and compliance**.
    - **Shortcuts to External Storage**: Users can connect to **Azure Data Lake Storage (ADLS), AWS S3, and on-premises data** without moving the data.
    - **Auto-Optimization and Caching**: Improves query performance for large-scale analytics.

    Think of OneLake as a "OneDrive for Data"—every dataset, whether structured or unstructured, is stored in a single, shared location for all teams.

CHAPTER 2   INTRODUCTION TO MICROSOFT FABRIC

3.2. Synapse-Powered Analytical Workloads

Microsoft Fabric integrates **Synapse Analytics** to power various workloads, enabling data professionals to perform diverse operations without switching between tools.

Core Workloads in Synapse

- **Data Engineering**: Uses Apache Spark to **process, clean, and transform large datasets** at scale.

- **Data Science**: Supports **Python, R, and AutoML** for **machine learning and AI-driven analytics**.

- **Data Warehousing**: Provides **SQL-based analytics** using **Synapse Data Warehousing**.

- **Real-Time Analytics**: Supports **streaming data ingestion and interactive querying using Kusto Query Language (KQL)**.

Synapse acts as the computational engine of Microsoft Fabric, ensuring fast, scalable, and cost-effective processing.

3.3. Data Integration Layer (Data Factory and Pipelines)

Microsoft Fabric includes a **revamped Data Factory** that allows seamless **ETL (Extract, Transform, Load) and ELT (Extract, Load, Transform) workflows**.

Key Features of Data Integration

- **Over 200 Pre-Built Connectors**: Connects to **SQL Server, SAP, Salesforce, Azure Blob Storage, and more**.

- **Low-Code Data Pipelines**: Drag-and-drop UI for building **complex data workflows**.
- **Incremental Data Loads**: Optimized for **batch processing and real-time ingestion**.
- **Dataflow Gen2**: A next-gen ETL tool optimized for **high-performance data preparation**.

With Fabric, data professionals can create automated workflows, ingest data from multiple sources, and perform large-scale transformations with ease.

3.4. Real-Time Analytics (Event Streams and KQL Databases)

Fabric provides **real-time data processing capabilities** using **Synapse Real-Time Analytics** and **Event Streams**.

Key Components

- **Event Streams**: Captures data from IoT devices, social media, logs, and sensors.
- **KQL (Kusto Query Language) Databases**: Used for **high-speed, ad hoc querying** of streaming data.
- **Low-Latency Data Processing**: Enables **fraud detection, anomaly detection, and operational monitoring** in real time.

Real-time analytics ensures organizations can react to data changes instantly, improving decision-making speed.

3.5. **Business Intelligence with Power BI**

Fabric tightly integrates **Power BI** to provide **self-service analytics, interactive dashboards, and AI-powered insights**.

Power BI Capabilities in Fabric

- **Direct Access to OneLake**: No need to copy/move data for report generation.
- **AI-Powered Insights**: Uses **Copilot AI** to generate **visualizations and summaries** automatically.
- **Row-Level Security (RLS)**: Ensures data privacy and access control.
- **Paginated Reports**: Supports **enterprise-level reporting needs**.

Power BI is the visualization and reporting layer of Fabric, making it easy for business users to interact with data.

3.6. **Security, Compliance, and Governance (Microsoft Purview Integration)**

Fabric is designed with **enterprise-grade security and governance**, ensuring compliance with global regulations.

Key Security Features

- **Microsoft Purview Integration**: Centralized governance for **data classification, lineage, and access control**.

- **Role-Based Access Control (RBAC)**: Restricts access based on user roles.
- **End-to-End Encryption**: Protects data at rest and in transit.
- **Multi-Factor Authentication (MFA)**: Adds extra security layers for authentication.
- **Compliance with GDPR, HIPAA, SOC 2**: Ensures regulatory adherence.

Fabric ensures organizations have full control over their data while maintaining the highest security standards.

3.7. Copilot AI and Automation

Fabric introduces **Copilot**, an AI-powered assistant that helps users

- **Generate Queries and Reports**: Users can type natural language prompts.
- **Automate Data Cleaning and Transformation**: AI suggests optimal ETL processes.
- **Predict Trends and Anomalies**: Machine learning-based forecasting.

Copilot helps both technical and nontechnical users derive insights from data quickly.

3.8. Scalability and Performance Optimization

Fabric is designed to scale seamlessly and optimize performance:

CHAPTER 2   INTRODUCTION TO MICROSOFT FABRIC

- **Serverless and Auto-Scaling**: Eliminates manual infrastructure management.
- **Multi-Cloud and Hybrid Support**: Works with Azure, AWS, and on-prem systems.
- **Optimized Query Engine**: Uses **Synapse and Delta Lake optimizations** for fast data retrieval.

Fabric ensures businesses can scale up and down efficiently without overpaying for resources.

Integrating Microsoft Fabric with Azure and Other Tools

1. **Introduction**

   Microsoft Fabric is designed as a unified **data analytics and business intelligence platform** that seamlessly integrates with **Azure services and other third-party tools**. This integration ensures that organizations can leverage their existing cloud infrastructure, optimize their data workflows, and enhance analytics capabilities without major disruptions.

   In this chapter, we explore **how Microsoft Fabric integrates with Azure services, third-party tools, and on-premises systems**, enabling businesses to create an **end-to-end data ecosystem**.

2. **Key Benefits of Integrating Fabric with Azure and Other Tools**

   Before diving into specific integrations, let's explore why **Fabric's interoperability with Azure and third-party solutions** is important:

   - **Seamless Dataflow**: Enables effortless movement of data between Azure services and Microsoft Fabric.
   - **Hybrid and Multi-Cloud Support**: Allows businesses to work across **Azure, AWS, Google Cloud, and on-premises environments**.
   - **Enhanced Security and Governance**: Leverages **Microsoft Purview and Azure Active Directory (AAD)** for **compliance, authentication, and access control**.
   - **Cost Optimization**: Fabric's integration with Azure allows organizations to **optimize cloud spending** by using serverless and auto-scaling capabilities.
   - **AI-Powered Insights**: Fabric integrates with **Azure AI/ML services** to enhance **data analytics and predictive modeling**.
   - **Automation and Orchestration**: Integration with **Azure Data Factory (ADF), Logic Apps, and Power Automate** helps streamline data workflows.

3. **Integrating Microsoft Fabric with Azure Services**

   Microsoft Fabric integrates **natively with various Azure services**, allowing users to access **data storage, compute, analytics, security, and AI functionalities**.

CHAPTER 2 INTRODUCTION TO MICROSOFT FABRIC

3.1. OneLake Integration with Azure Data Services

Since **OneLake** is at the core of Microsoft Fabric, it is **designed to integrate effortlessly with Azure storage solutions**.

Connecting OneLake with Azure Data Lake Storage Gen2 (ADLS Gen2)

- OneLake **supports direct connections** to **ADLS Gen2**, allowing organizations to **access and analyze data** without needing to move it.
- Users can **create shortcuts** to ADLS Gen2 containers, ensuring that **data duplication is minimized**.

Integration with Azure Blob Storage

- Fabric enables **data ingestion from Azure Blob Storage** into **Lakehouses, Warehouses, and Real-Time Analytics**.
- Supports **incremental and full loads** from **Blob Storage to Fabric workloads**.

Integration with Azure SQL and Synapse Analytics

- Microsoft Fabric **natively connects** to **Azure SQL Database, SQL Server, and Synapse Analytics**.
- Data can be **federated between Fabric's SQL-based Warehouses and Azure Synapse**.
- **T-SQL compatibility** ensures **easy migration** of queries from Azure SQL to Fabric's **Lakehouse and Warehouse environments**.

3.2. Data Engineering and ETL with Azure Data Factory

Microsoft Fabric **seamlessly integrates with Azure Data Factory (ADF) for data ingestion, transformation, and orchestration.**

Key Features of Azure Data Factory Integration

- **Over 200 Pre-Built Connectors**: Easily connect to **Azure services, databases, SaaS applications, and third-party tools**.
- **ETL/ELT Pipeline Automation**: Enables **scheduled data movement** between Azure and Fabric.
- **Low-Code and No-Code Dataflows**: Users can build **complex data transformation pipelines** without writing code.
- **Hybrid and On-Prem Connectivity**: Supports **Azure Data Gateway** for securely pulling data from **on-premises sources**.

Example: A company using **SAP on-premises** can extract data using **Azure Data Factory**, transform it, and load it into **Microsoft Fabric for analysis**.

3.3. Real-Time Data Processing with Azure Event Hub and IoT Hub

Microsoft Fabric enables **real-time analytics** by integrating with **Azure Event Hub and IoT Hub**.

How Real-Time Data is Integrated into Fabric?

- **Event Hub** streams **real-time telemetry data** into **Fabric's Kusto Query Language (KQL) databases**.

- **IoT Hub** captures **sensor and device data** and sends it to Fabric's **Event Streams or Data Warehouse**.

- **Fabric's Real-Time Analytics Engine** allows for **real-time monitoring, anomaly detection, and predictive analytics**.

Example: A **smart manufacturing company** can stream sensor data from **Azure IoT Hub** into **Fabric's Real-Time Analytics** for **predictive maintenance**.

3.4. **AI and Machine Learning Integration with Azure AI and Synapse ML**

Fabric allows **seamless AI and ML integration** with **Azure AI and Synapse ML**, enabling organizations to **derive intelligent insights from data**.

Key AI/ML Integrations

- **Azure Machine Learning (Azure ML)**: Train and deploy ML models directly on Fabric's **Lakehouse data**.

- **Synapse ML (Machine Learning for Big Data)**: Run **distributed ML pipelines** using **Spark and Fabric Data Science Notebooks**.

- **Microsoft Copilot AI**: Uses **natural language queries to generate insights, reports, and code recommendations**.

- **Azure OpenAI Service**: Integrates with **ChatGPT and GPT-powered services** to provide AI-driven analytics.

Example: A **retail company** can use **Azure ML** with **Fabric Lakehouse data** to create a **customer churn prediction model**.

3.5. Security and Governance with Microsoft Purview and Azure AD

Fabric integrates with **Microsoft Purview** and **Azure Active Directory (AAD)** to ensure **robust security and compliance**.

Security Features

- **Single Sign-On (SSO) with Azure AD**: Ensures secure authentication for users.
- **Role-Based Access Control (RBAC)**: Assigns different levels of access to users based on roles.
- **Data Lineage and Governance (Purview)**: Tracks **data movement and transformation** across Fabric and Azure.
- **Encryption and Compliance**: Supports **GDPR, HIPAA, SOC 2 compliance standards**.

Example: A **financial institution** using Fabric can enforce **data access policies** with **Azure AD and Microsoft Purview**.

4. **Integrating Microsoft Fabric with Third-Party Tools**

   Microsoft Fabric is **not limited to Azure**—it can also integrate with **third-party applications, BI tools, and databases**.

CHAPTER 2   INTRODUCTION TO MICROSOFT FABRIC

4.1. **Integration with AWS and Google Cloud**

- **Fabric allows connections to AWS S3 buckets and Google BigQuery** via OneLake shortcuts.
- **Supports multi-cloud analytics pipelines using Azure Data Factory.**

4.2. **Integration with Popular BI Tools**

Although **Fabric natively integrates with Power BI**, it also supports

- **Tableau**
- **Looker (Google Data Studio)**
- **QlikView**

4.3. **Integration with SaaS Applications**

- **Fabric connects with Salesforce, SAP, ServiceNow, and Microsoft 365 apps.**
- **Data Factory Pipelines** help extract, transform, and load SaaS data into **Fabric Lakehouse/Warehouse**.

Example: A **marketing team** can pull customer data from **Salesforce into Fabric Lakehouse**, apply ML models, and create interactive reports in **Power BI**.

Chapter Summary

In this chapter, we have explored the unified data analytics capabilities of Microsoft Fabric, a powerful platform that seamlessly integrates Power BI, Synapse, Data Factory, and AI services to deliver end-to-end data solutions.

CHAPTER 2   INTRODUCTION TO MICROSOFT FABRIC

We began by understanding how this unified platform supports data engineering, real-time analytics, and AI-driven insights within a single ecosystem. This empowers organizations to accelerate decision-making by connecting data from multiple sources into one coherent pipeline.

We examined the foundational role of OneLake, the centralized data lake for all Fabric workloads, which allows for simplified data storage, management, and sharing across the organization. Readers learn how this eliminates silos and ensures a single version of truth across all data activities.

The Lakehouse architecture was discussed as a modern data solution that bridges the gap between data lakes and data warehouses, supporting both structured and unstructured data. This provides flexibility to data engineers and data scientists alike.

We also covered the data movement and transformation layer, powered by Data Pipelines, Dataflows, and Azure Data Factory, which enables robust ETL/ELT operations. Readers understand how they can automate data ingestion, cleansing, and transformation for downstream analytics.

The integration of AI and machine learning capabilities, including Copilot, Azure AI, and SynapseML, was highlighted to demonstrate how intelligent analytics and predictive modeling can be embedded directly into data workflows.

We emphasized scalability and performance, showcasing features like serverless compute and automatic optimization, which help deliver high-speed processing without manual resource provisioning.

For data security and governance, we explored how Microsoft Purview and Azure Active Directory ensure compliance, access control, and data lineage—crucial for regulated industries and enterprise deployments.

Additionally, we discussed the Real-Time Analytics feature powered by Kusto Query Language (KQL), which supports instant insights from streaming data sources—a major asset for time-sensitive decision-making.

CHAPTER 2 INTRODUCTION TO MICROSOFT FABRIC

The native integration with Power BI provides seamless visualization capabilities, enabling users to create interactive dashboards and reports without moving data across platforms.

We further examined the interoperability with Azure services such as Data Lake, Synapse Analytics, Event Hub, and Azure Machine Learning, allowing organizations to extend Fabric's functionality as needed.

The platform's hybrid support, via Data Gateway, enables secure data access from on-premises and multi-cloud environments, ensuring flexibility in deployment strategies.

Lastly, we looked at the support for third-party tools like Tableau, Looker, AWS S3, and Google BigQuery, which ensures that Microsoft Fabric fits well into diverse enterprise ecosystems.

By the end of this chapter, readers will have gained a comprehensive understanding of how Microsoft Fabric acts as an all-in-one platform for modern data analytics—bridging gaps across data engineering, storage, governance, visualization, and AI. This equips professionals with the knowledge to build scalable, intelligent, and collaborative data solutions.

CHAPTER 3

Implement a Data Warehouse with Microsoft Fabric

Chapter Overview

Data warehousing is a fundamental aspect of enterprise analytics, enabling organizations to store, process, and analyze vast amounts of structured and semi-structured data. Microsoft Fabric provides a powerful and unified analytics platform that simplifies data warehouse implementation by integrating data engineering, storage, and analytics capabilities in a single environment.

In this chapter, readers will explore the end-to-end process of implementing a data warehouse within Microsoft Fabric. The chapter begins with an introduction to setting up a data warehouse, discussing architectural considerations and best practices for deployment. Readers will then delve into **data modeling concepts**, understanding schema design, relationships, and optimization techniques for efficient querying.

CHAPTER 3 IMPLEMENT A DATA WAREHOUSE WITH MICROSOFT FABRIC

Next, the **ETL (Extract, Transform, Load) process** will be covered, guiding readers through data ingestion, transformation workflows, and automation strategies using Microsoft Fabric's Data Factory, Spark, and other built-in tools. Finally, the chapter will focus on **managing data storage and performance**, ensuring efficient data retrieval, indexing, partitioning, and cost-effective storage utilization within the platform.

By the end of this chapter, readers will be equipped with the knowledge and practical skills to implement a robust data warehouse in Microsoft Fabric, leveraging its capabilities for scalable and high-performance analytics.

Key Terms

- **Microsoft Fabric**: A unified analytics platform integrating data engineering, data science, real-time analytics, and business intelligence.

- **OneLake**: A centralized storage layer in Microsoft Fabric that unifies data across different services.

- **Data Warehouse**: A structured repository designed for analytical processing and reporting.

- **Lakehouse**: A hybrid storage architecture that combines the benefits of data lakes and data warehouses.

- **Fabric SQL Endpoints**: T-SQL-supported query interfaces for accessing data in Fabric Data Warehouses and Lakehouses.

- **T-SQL (Transact-SQL)**: A Microsoft SQL Server query language used for managing and manipulating data.

- **Power BI Integration**: The ability of Fabric to connect seamlessly with Power BI for reporting and visualization.

- **Azure Synapse Analytics**: A cloud-based analytics service that works with Fabric for big data and machine learning.

- **Star Schema**: A data modeling approach with a central fact table linked to multiple dimension tables.

- **Snowflake Schema**: A normalized form of Star Schema where dimensions are further divided into subdimensions.

- **Fact Table**: Stores measurable business data, such as sales transactions or revenue.

- **Dimension Table**: Contains descriptive attributes about business entities, such as customers, products, or time.

- **Slowly Changing Dimensions (SCDs)**: A method for managing changes in dimension tables over time.

- **SCD Type 1**: Overwrites old data with new values, losing historical records.

- **SCD Type 2**: Maintains historical versions of data by adding new rows with timestamps.

- **SCD Type 3**: Stores both the previous and current values in the same row.

- **SCD Type 4**: Keeps historical data in a separate table for reference.

- **SCD Type 6**: A hybrid approach combining elements of SCD Type 1, 2, and 3.

- **Surrogate Key**: A system-generated unique identifier used instead of natural keys for better performance.

- **Natural Key**: A real-world identifier (e.g., email, SSN) used to uniquely identify records.

- **ETL (Extract, Transform, Load)**: A process where data is extracted from sources, transformed, and then loaded into a warehouse.

- **ELT (Extract, Load, Transform)**: A variation where raw data is first loaded into storage and then transformed inside the warehouse.

- **Dataflows**: A Power BI tool for automating ETL processes using a graphical interface.

- **Data Factory Pipelines**: Azure-based workflows for ingesting, transforming, and moving data across services.

- **Notebooks and Spark**: Tools used in Fabric for processing and analyzing large datasets, often using Python.

- **Delta Tables**: Optimized tables in Fabric that support ACID transactions and fast processing.

- **Incremental Data Loading**: A technique where only new or changed data is processed instead of reloading everything.

- **Bulk Insert Operations**: A method for inserting large volumes of data efficiently into a database.

- **Partitioning**: Dividing large tables into smaller, manageable sections to improve performance.

- **Range Partitioning**: A type of partitioning where data is divided based on a range of values (e.g., date).

- **Hash Distribution**: A method of distributing data across storage nodes based on a hash function.

- **Clustered Columnstore Index**: A storage and indexing technique optimized for high-performance analytics queries.

- **Non-Clustered Index**: A secondary index that speeds up lookups for specific queries.

- **Materialized Views**: Precomputed query results stored for faster retrieval and performance optimization.

- **Query Optimization**: Techniques used to improve the efficiency of database queries.

- **Query Execution Plans**: Visual or textual representations of how a database engine processes a query.

- **Performance Monitoring**: The process of tracking system performance using tools like logs and dashboards.

- **Azure Monitor**: A service for collecting and analyzing performance data across Azure resources.

- **Fabric Query History**: A feature in Fabric that logs executed queries for analysis and troubleshooting.

- **Storage Optimization**: Techniques for managing and optimizing data storage to reduce costs and improve performance.

- **Partition Pruning**: A query optimization technique that limits scans to relevant partitions, improving performance.

Setting Up a Data Warehouse in Microsoft Fabric

Implementing a data warehouse in **Microsoft Fabric** involves several key steps, from environment setup to defining data structures and configuring security. This section provides a step-by-step guide to setting up a data warehouse, ensuring a scalable, efficient, and well-optimized analytics solution.

1. **Understanding Microsoft Fabric Data Warehousing**

    Microsoft Fabric provides a **unified data platform** that integrates **data engineering, data warehousing, and analytics** into a seamless environment. The Fabric Data Warehouse is **built on a distributed processing architecture** that supports massive scalability, real-time analytics, and easy integration with Microsoft services such as Power BI, Azure Synapse Analytics, and Microsoft Purview. Figure 3-1 shows the warehouse option in Fabric.

CHAPTER 3   IMPLEMENT A DATA WAREHOUSE WITH MICROSOFT FABRIC

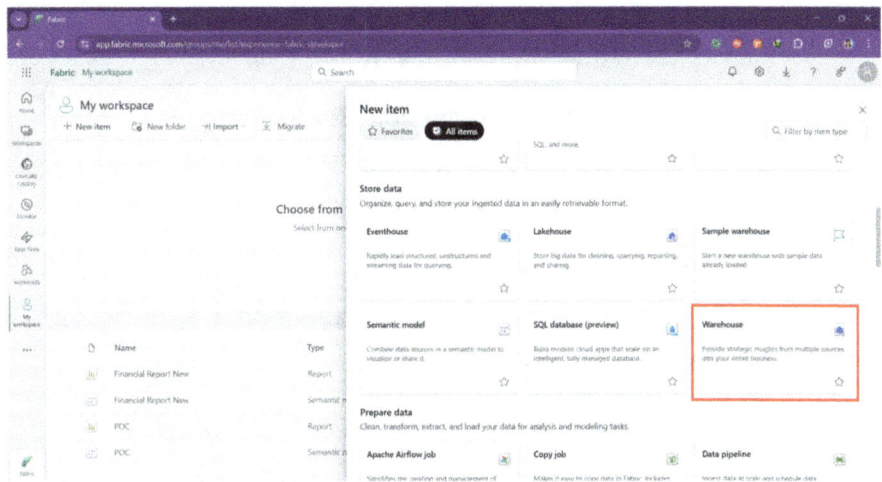

Figure 3-1. *Data warehouse in Fabric*

Key Features of Microsoft Fabric Data Warehouse

- **Cloud-native and Serverless**: No infrastructure management, auto-scaling, and cost optimization.

- **Lakehouse and Warehouse Integration**: Seamless connectivity between structured (SQL-based) and unstructured (Lakehouse) data.

- **Built-in Security and Compliance**: Role-based access control, encryption, and integration with Microsoft Purview for governance.

- **Optimized for Performance**: Uses **Direct Lake mode**, indexing, and caching for faster query performance.

2. **Setting Up the Data Warehouse Environment**
   Step 1: Accessing Microsoft Fabric

   To start setting up a data warehouse in Fabric, you need access to **Microsoft Fabric** via the Power BI portal or Microsoft Fabric Admin Center.

   Prerequisites

   - A **Microsoft Fabric-enabled tenant** (check in the Power BI admin portal).
   - A **Premium Capacity workspace** to utilize full data warehousing features.

   Steps to Enable Fabric

   1. Log in to **Microsoft Fabric** via Power BI Portal (https://app.fabric.microsoft.com/).
   2. Navigate to the **Admin Portal** ➤ Click **Fabric** settings.
   3. Ensure that **Data Warehouse** and **Lakehouse** features are enabled.
   4. Assign users and roles to access **Fabric Data Warehouse**.

CHAPTER 3   IMPLEMENT A DATA WAREHOUSE WITH MICROSOFT FABRIC

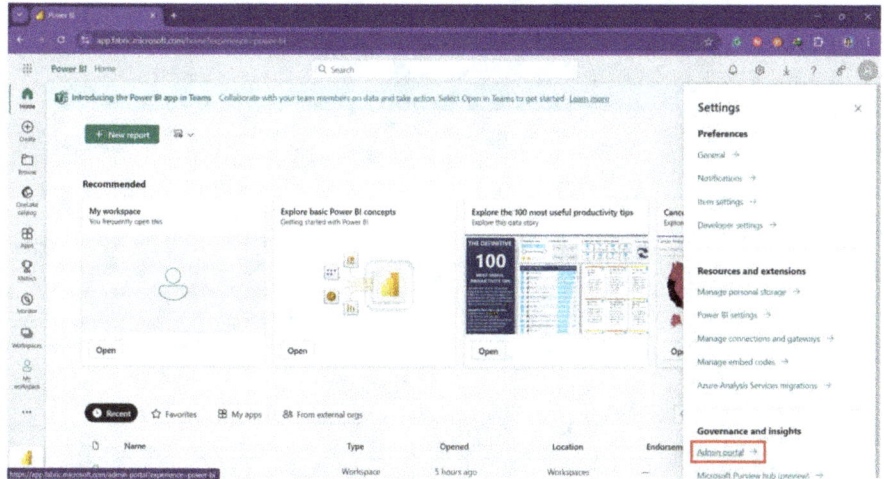

Figure 3-2. *Microsoft Admin Portal*

3. **Creating a Data Warehouse in Microsoft Fabric**

   Once Fabric is enabled, you can create a **Data Warehouse as shown in Figure 3-3 inside a Fabric workspace.**

   Step 1: Creating a Warehouse

   1. **Go to Fabric Portal** ➤ Select a **Workspace**.

   2. Click **New** ➤ Choose **Warehouse**.

   3. Provide a **name** for your warehouse.

   4. Click **Create**.

81

CHAPTER 3   IMPLEMENT A DATA WAREHOUSE WITH MICROSOFT FABRIC

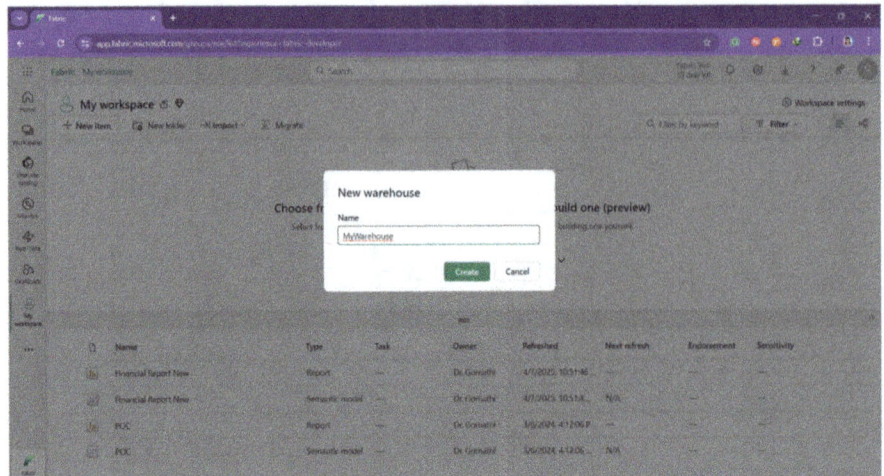

Figure 3-3. *Name the warehouse*

Step 2: Configuring Data Warehouse Settings

- **Define Storage Location**: Choose **OneLake** as your unified data storage.

- **Set Up Compute and Scaling Options**: Microsoft Fabric auto-scales based on workload.

- **Assign Security and Permissions**: Use **Azure Active Directory (AAD)** for access control.

4. **Connecting to Data Sources**

Step 1: Ingesting Data into the Warehouse

Data can be ingested from multiple sources such as

- **Azure Data Factory**: Automate ETL pipelines for structured data.

- **OneLake and Lakehouse**: Unified storage for semi-structured data.

- **SQL Databases (On-Prem and Cloud)**: Use Linked Services for live connections.
- **Microsoft Dataverse, Dynamics 365, and Power Platform**: Direct integration.

Step 2: Loading Data Using SQL Queries

Once data sources are connected, load data using SQL statements:

```
CREATE TABLE SalesData (
    SaleID INT PRIMARY KEY,
    ProductName VARCHAR(100),
    SaleAmount DECIMAL(10,2),
    SaleDate DATE
);

INSERT INTO SalesData (SaleID, ProductName, SaleAmount, SaleDate)
VALUES (1, 'Laptop', 1200.50, '2025-03-10');
```

Best Practices

- Use **staging tables** for raw data before transformation.
- Partition large tables for **faster queries**.
- Optimize indexes for **better performance**.

5. **Configuring Security and Governance**

Step 1: Setting Up Role-Based Access Control (RBAC)

Fabric uses **Azure Active Directory (AAD)** for managing access.

- **Workspace Admins**: Full control over the data warehouse.
- **Data Engineers**: Can create tables, modify schemas, and manage ETL.
- **Analysts**: Can run queries but cannot modify schema.

Use the following SQL to grant permissions:

```
GRANT SELECT ON SalesData TO AnalystRole;
GRANT INSERT, UPDATE, DELETE ON SalesData TO DataEngineerRole;
```

Step 2: Implementing Data Governance with Microsoft Purview

- Define **data lineage** and **sensitivity labels** to track data movement.
- Use **row-level security (RLS)** to restrict access based on user roles.

6. **Optimizing Performance and Storage**

   Storage Optimization Strategies

   - **Use OneLake for Unified Storage**: Ensures faster data retrieval.
   - **Partition Large Tables**: Improve query performance for big datasets.
   - **Enable Caching and Indexing**: Reduce query execution time.

Performance Optimization Techniques

- Use **Direct Lake mode** instead of Import mode for better speed.
- Optimize queries using **materialized views** for repeated reports.
- Monitor performance using **SQL Query Performance Insights** in Fabric.

Data Modeling Concepts in Microsoft Fabric

Introduction to Data Modeling in Microsoft Fabric

Data modeling is the process of defining how data is **structured, stored, and related** within a data warehouse. A well-designed **data model** ensures **efficient querying, storage optimization, and better analytics performance**. In Microsoft Fabric, data modeling plays a crucial role in transforming raw data into a meaningful, structured format for analytics and reporting.

This section explores **data modeling best practices** in Microsoft Fabric, including **schema design, normalization vs. denormalization, relationships, indexing, and performance optimization**. It also aligns with key concepts from the **DP-600: Implementing Analytics Solutions Using Microsoft Fabric** certification, ensuring readers are well-prepared for the exam.

1. **Understanding Data Modeling in Fabric Data Warehouse**

    Microsoft Fabric provides multiple data storage options, each suited for different workloads:

Storage Option	Description	Use Case
Data Warehouse	Structured, relational data optimized for SQL queries.	Large-scale enterprise reporting.
Lakehouse	Combines structured (SQL tables) and unstructured (files, parquet).	Big data analytics.
KQL Databases	Optimized for log and time-series analytics.	Real-time monitoring, IoT, logs.
Dataverse	Low-code data storage for Power Platform.	Power Apps and Dynamics 365.

For enterprise analytics, **Data Warehouses** and **Lakehouses** are the primary storage options for structured data.

2. **Core Data Modeling Concepts**

    2.1. **Star Schema vs. Snowflake Schema**

    The two most common **schema designs** in data warehousing are

    Star Schema (Recommended for Fabric)

    A **star schema** consists of a **fact table** connected to multiple **dimension tables**, ensuring faster queries and efficient analytics.

    Advantages

    - Simpler and faster queries.
    - Optimized for **Power BI and Fabric Direct Lake mode**.
    - Easy to scale for large datasets.

Example

- **Fact Table**: SalesData (Transaction Amount, Date, Product ID, Customer ID)

- **Dimension Tables**: Customers, Products, Date, Region

```
CREATE TABLE SalesData (
    SaleID INT PRIMARY KEY,
    ProductID INT,
    CustomerID INT,
    SaleAmount DECIMAL(10,2),
    SaleDate DATE,
    FOREIGN KEY (ProductID) REFERENCES
    Products(ProductID),
    FOREIGN KEY (CustomerID) REFERENCES
    Customers(CustomerID)
);
```

2.2. Snowflake Schema (Normalized Schema)

A **snowflake schema** is a more normalized version of a star schema, where **dimension tables** are further split into subdimensions to eliminate redundancy.

Advantages

- Reduces **data duplication**
- Improves **storage efficiency**

Disadvantages

- More complex queries due to **multiple joins**
- Not ideal for **Fabric Direct Lake mode**, as joins impact performance

Example

Instead of a single **Customers** table, it can be broken down into CustomerDetails, CustomerLocation, etc.

```
CREATE TABLE CustomerDetails (
    CustomerID INT PRIMARY KEY,
    CustomerName VARCHAR(100),
    ContactNumber VARCHAR(15)
);

CREATE TABLE CustomerLocation (
    LocationID INT PRIMARY KEY,
    CustomerID INT,
    City VARCHAR(50),
    Country VARCHAR(50),
    FOREIGN KEY (CustomerID) REFERENCES
    CustomerDetails(CustomerID)
);
```

Best Practice: Use Star Schema in Microsoft Fabric for **optimized query performance** in Power BI and Direct Lake mode.

3. **Fact and Dimension Tables**

   3.1. **Fact Tables (Transaction Data)**

   - Contain **measurable, numerical data** (e.g., sales, revenue, transactions).
   - Linked to **dimension tables** through foreign keys.

Example: Sales transactions, Order details, Revenue.

```
CREATE TABLE FactSales (
    SaleID INT PRIMARY KEY,
    ProductID INT,
    CustomerID INT,
    SaleAmount DECIMAL(10,2),
    SaleDate DATE
);
```

3.2. Dimension Tables (Descriptive Data)

- Contain **descriptive attributes** (e.g., Customer Name, Product Category).
- Used for filtering and grouping in reports.

Example: Customer demographics, Product details, Dates.

```
CREATE TABLE DimCustomers (
    CustomerID INT PRIMARY KEY,
    CustomerName VARCHAR(100),
    Region VARCHAR(50)
);
```

4. Data Normalization vs. Denormalization

4.1. Normalization (3NF, Snowflake Schema)

- Reduces **redundancy** and improves **data integrity**
- Ensures **data consistency** across tables
- Requires **more joins**, affecting query performance

Use Case: Transaction systems, operational databases

4.2. Denormalization (Star Schema)

- **Pre-joins data**, reducing query complexity
- Improves **performance** in Fabric and Power BI
- Increases **redundancy**, but speeds up reporting

Use Case: Data Warehouses, Power BI reports

5. Relationships and Indexing for Optimized Query Performance

5.1. Defining Primary and Foreign Keys

To enforce **data integrity, always define primary keys (PK) and foreign keys (FK)** in your schema.

```
ALTER TABLE FactSales ADD CONSTRAINT FK_Product FOREIGN KEY (ProductID) REFERENCES DimProducts(ProductID);
```

5.2. Indexing Strategies in Fabric

Indexes **speed up query performance** but require careful management.

- **Use clustered indexes for large tables.**

    ```
    CREATE CLUSTERED INDEX idx_sales ON FactSales (SaleDate);
    ```

- **Use non-clustered indexes for high-selectivity columns.**

    ```
    CREATE NONCLUSTERED INDEX idx_product ON
    FactSales (ProductID);
    ```

6. **Performance Optimization in Fabric Data Warehouse (DP-600 Key Points)**

    6.1. **Use Direct Lake Mode for Power BI**

    - **Direct Lake Mode** bypasses import mode and speeds up Power BI reports.
    - Recommended over **Direct Query** for large datasets.

    6.2. **Partition Large Tables**

    Partitioning **improves query speed** by breaking large tables into smaller segments.

    ```
    ALTER TABLE FactSales PARTITION BY RANGE
    (SaleDate);
    ```

    Best for: Tables with millions of rows (e.g., sales data).

    6.3. **Use Materialized Views for Precomputed Aggregates**

    Materialized views store **precomputed results**, reducing query time.

    ```
    CREATE MATERIALIZED VIEW SalesSummary AS
    SELECT ProductID, SUM(SaleAmount) AS TotalSales
    FROM FactSales GROUP BY ProductID;
    ```

CHAPTER 3   IMPLEMENT A DATA WAREHOUSE WITH MICROSOFT FABRIC

6.4. **Implement Row-Level Security (RLS)**

Restrict **data access** based on user roles.

```
CREATE SECURITY POLICY SalesPolicy
ADD FILTER PREDICATE UserRegion = 'East' ON
FactSales;
```

Understanding **data modeling** is crucial for **high-performance analytics in Microsoft Fabric**. A well-designed schema **improves query speed, enhances storage efficiency, and ensures data integrity**.

- **Star Schema is recommended** for Fabric Data Warehouse.
- **Use Indexing, Partitioning, and Materialized Views** for optimization.
- **Direct Lake mode enhances Power BI performance**.
- **Follow DP-600 best practices for scalability and efficiency**.

In the next section, we will explore the **ETL Process in Microsoft Fabric**, covering **data ingestion, transformation, and automation techniques**.

ETL Process with Microsoft Fabric

Introduction to ETL in Microsoft Fabric
The **ETL (Extract, Transform, Load) process** is fundamental in **data engineering and analytics**, enabling organizations to move, clean, and transform raw data into structured and meaningful insights. In **Microsoft Fabric**, ETL is optimized using **Data Pipelines, Dataflows, Data Factory, Notebooks, and Lakehouses**, ensuring a seamless integration between data sources, transformations, and destinations.

This section explores the **ETL process in Microsoft Fabric**, covering best practices, **Data Factory Pipelines, Apache Spark transformations, and Delta Lake storage**, aligning with the **DP-600: Microsoft Certified Fabric Analytics Engineer Associate** certification.

1. **ETL vs. ELT: Choosing the Right Approach**
   Traditionally, **ETL** (Extract, Transform, Load) was the primary approach, but with **modern cloud data platforms** like Fabric, **ELT** (Extract, Load, Transform) is preferred for scalability and performance.

Approach	Description	Use Case
ETL	Data is **transformed before loading** into the data warehouse.	When data cleansing and business rules must be applied before storage.
ELT	Data is **loaded first** into Fabric Lakehouse, then transformed using SQL or Spark.	When dealing with **big data** or structured/unstructured data.

   Best Practice in Microsoft Fabric: Use **ELT with Lakehouse** and **Data Pipelines** for large-scale analytics.

2. **Extracting Data in Microsoft Fabric**

   2.1. **Connecting to Data Sources**

   Fabric supports a **wide range of data sources** for extraction, including

- **Databases**: SQL Server, Azure Synapse, PostgreSQL, MySQL

- **Cloud Storage**: Azure Data Lake, AWS S3, Google Cloud Storage

- **Business Applications**: Dynamics 365, Salesforce, SAP

- **Files**: CSV, JSON, Parquet, Excel

2.2. **Using Data Factory Pipelines for Extraction**

Microsoft Fabric provides **Data Pipelines** (similar to Azure Data Factory) to connect, ingest, and orchestrate data movement.

Example: Extracting data from SQL Server into Fabric Data Warehouse

```
COPY INTO FactSales
FROM 'https://storagesample.blob.core.windows.net/salesdata.csv'
WITH (
    FILE_TYPE = 'CSV',
    FIELDTERMINATOR = ',',
    ROWTERMINATOR = '\n'
);
```

Best Practice: Use **Incremental Loads** to process only new data instead of full loads.

3. **Transforming Data in Microsoft Fabric**

Transformation ensures that **raw data is cleaned, standardized, and structured** for analytics.

CHAPTER 3   IMPLEMENT A DATA WAREHOUSE WITH MICROSOFT FABRIC

3.1. Data Cleansing and Standardization

- Remove duplicates, handle missing values.
- Convert data types (e.g., Date format standardization).
- Enrich data (e.g., adding calculated columns).

Example: Using Spark Notebooks to Clean Data

```
from pyspark.sql.functions import col, trim

# Load Data from Lakehouse
df = spark.read.format("delta").load("lakehouse/fact_sales")

# Data Cleaning
df_cleaned = df.withColumn("CustomerName", trim(col("CustomerName"))).dropna()

# Save back to Lakehouse
df_cleaned.write.format("delta").mode("overwrite").save("lakehouse/fact_sales_cleaned")
```

Best Practice: Use **Apache Spark Notebooks** for complex transformations at scale.

3.2. Implementing Slowly Changing Dimensions (SCDs)

In a **data warehouse**, tracking historical changes in dimension tables is critical. In a **data warehouse**, a **dimension table** stores **descriptive attributes** (such as customer details, product descriptions, or employee information). Over time, these attributes change. Managing these changes efficiently while preserving data integrity is crucial.

CHAPTER 3   IMPLEMENT A DATA WAREHOUSE WITH MICROSOFT FABRIC

Slowly Changing Dimensions (SCDs) define **how historical changes in dimension attributes** should be handled. Microsoft Fabric supports **various types of SCD implementations**, depending on business requirements.

Types of Slowly Changing Dimensions (SCDs)

There are **six types** of SCDs, each with a unique approach to handling changes in dimension data.

SCD Type	Description	Example	Implementation Complexity
SCD Type 0	No changes allowed; data remains static.	A product category that never changes.	Low
SCD Type 1	Overwrites old data with new values.	Updating a customer's phone number.	Low
SCD Type 2	Creates a new record with historical tracking.	Keeping track of address changes over time.	Medium
SCD Type 3	Stores a limited history (previous value).	Keeping the last and current employer of an employee.	Medium
SCD Type 4	Maintains a history table and a current table.	Maintaining all customer address changes in a separate table.	High
SCD Type 6	Combines SCD Types 1, 2, and 3 for full historical tracking.	Storing current and previous values while maintaining a full history.	High

SCD Type 0: Fixed Attributes (No Change Allowed)

- Data **remains unchanged** once inserted.
- Any attempt to modify the data is **rejected or ignored**.
- Used for **historical data that should not change**.

Use Case

- Product categories (e.g., "Electronics," "Furniture")
- National identification numbers (e.g., Social Security Number)

Implementation: Enforce constraints at the **database level** (e.g., using CHECK constraints or read-only settings).

SCD Type 1: Overwriting Data (No History Preserved)

- Old data is **replaced with new data**, without maintaining history.
- Simple but **does not track changes** over time.

Use Case

- Updating **customer contact information** (e.g., phone number, email)

Implementation in SQL (Fabric Data Warehouse)

```
UPDATE DimCustomer
SET PhoneNumber = '9876543210'
WHERE CustomerID = 101;
```

Pros: Simple, saves storage

Cons: No historical tracking of changes

SCD Type 2: Historical Tracking with New Records

- Maintains historical data by **creating a new row** for each change
- Uses **Effective Date, Expiry Date, and Active Flag** to differentiate records
- Allows users to **see past data versions**

Use Case

- Tracking **customer address changes over time**

Implementation in SQL (Fabric Data Warehouse)

```
MERGE INTO DimCustomer AS Target
USING StagingCustomer AS Source
ON Target.CustomerID = Source.CustomerID
WHEN MATCHED AND Target.Address <> Source.Address
THEN UPDATE SET Target.ValidTo = GETDATE(),
Target.IsActive = 0
WHEN NOT MATCHED
```

CHAPTER 3 IMPLEMENT A DATA WAREHOUSE WITH MICROSOFT FABRIC

```
THEN INSERT (CustomerID, CustomerName, Address,
ValidFrom, ValidTo, IsActive)
VALUES (Source.CustomerID, Source.CustomerName,
Source.Address, GETDATE(), NULL, 1);
```

Pros: Full historical tracking

Cons: More storage required, increased complexity

SCD Type 3: Storing Previous and Current Values

- **Limited history tracking** by adding **new columns** (e.g., "Previous Address").
- Only the **most recent change** is tracked.

Use Case

- Tracking **last and current employer** of an employee

Implementation in SQL (Fabric Data Warehouse)

```
UPDATE DimEmployee
SET PreviousEmployer = CurrentEmployer,
    CurrentEmployer = 'Microsoft'
WHERE EmployeeID = 201;
```

Pros: Saves space, provides some history

Cons: Limited history (cannot track multiple changes)

SCD Type 4: History Table and Current Table

- Maintains **two tables**:
  1. **Current table** (stores only the latest record)
  2. **Historical table** (tracks all changes)

Use Case

- Keeping **detailed historical records of customer address changes**

Implementation in SQL (Fabric Data Warehouse)

Step 1: Creating Tables

```
CREATE TABLE DimCustomer_Current (
    CustomerID INT PRIMARY KEY,
    CustomerName VARCHAR(100),
    Address VARCHAR(200)
);

CREATE TABLE DimCustomer_History (
    CustomerID INT,
    CustomerName VARCHAR(100),
    Address VARCHAR(200),
    ChangeDate DATETIME
);
```

Step 2: Updating Records

```
INSERT INTO DimCustomer_History
SELECT *, GETDATE() FROM DimCustomer_Current WHERE CustomerID = 101;
```

CHAPTER 3　IMPLEMENT A DATA WAREHOUSE WITH MICROSOFT FABRIC

```
UPDATE DimCustomer_Current
SET Address = 'New Street, NY' WHERE
CustomerID = 101;
```

Pros: Full history tracking with a separate archive

Cons: More complex querying across tables

SCD Type 6: Hybrid Approach (Combination of Types 1, 2, and 3)

Stores **current data, previous value, and full history**

- Combination of **SCD Type 1 (overwrite), Type 2 (new records), and Type 3 (previous columns)**

Use Case

- Tracking **customer address history while keeping current and previous address**

Implementation in SQL (Fabric Data Warehouse)

```
ALTER TABLE DimCustomer ADD PreviousAddress VARCHAR(200);
MERGE INTO DimCustomer AS Target
USING StagingCustomer AS Source
ON Target.CustomerID = Source.CustomerID
WHEN MATCHED AND Target.Address <> Source.Address
THEN UPDATE
SET Target.PreviousAddress = Target.Address,
    Target.Address = Source.Address,
    Target.ValidTo = GETDATE(),
    Target.IsActive = 0;
```

```
WHEN NOT MATCHED
THEN INSERT (CustomerID, CustomerName, Address,
PreviousAddress, ValidFrom, ValidTo, IsActive)
VALUES (Source.CustomerID, Source.CustomerName,
Source.Address, NULL, GETDATE(), NULL, 1);
```

Pros: Tracks full history while maintaining an easy-to-query structure

Cons: Higher storage and maintenance complexity

Best Practices for Implementing SCDs in Microsoft Fabric

- **Use SCD Type 2 for full history tracking in data warehouses.**
- **Use SCD Type 1 when history is not needed and performance is critical.**
- **Use SCD Type 3 for tracking a single previous value.**
- **Use SCD Type 4 when historical tracking is needed in a separate table.**
- **Use SCD Type 6 when both history and previous/current values are required.**
- **Implement indexing and partitioning** in Fabric Data Warehouse for performance optimization.

Example: Implementing SCD Type 2 in Fabric SQL

```sql
MERGE INTO DimCustomer AS target
USING StagingCustomer AS source
ON target.CustomerID = source.CustomerID
WHEN MATCHED AND target.CustomerAddress <>
source.CustomerAddress
THEN UPDATE SET target.ValidTo = GETDATE()
WHEN NOT MATCHED THEN
INSERT (CustomerID, CustomerName, CustomerAddress,
ValidFrom, ValidTo)
VALUES (source.CustomerID, source.CustomerName,
source.CustomerAddress, GETDATE(), NULL);
```

Best Practice: Use **MERGE statements** to handle **SCD updates efficiently**.

3.3. Aggregation and Preprocessing for Performance Optimization

- **Materialized Views** for precomputed aggregations.
- **Partitioning large tables** for faster queries.

```sql
CREATE MATERIALIZED VIEW SalesSummary AS

SELECT ProductID, SUM(SaleAmount) AS TotalSales
FROM FactSales GROUP BY ProductID;
```

Best Practice: Optimize **query performance** by **precomputing aggregates**.

4. **Loading Data in Microsoft Fabric**

   4.1. **Loading Data into Fabric Data Warehouse**

   Once data is transformed, it needs to be loaded into a **structured format** for analytics.

   Example: Bulk Load into Fabric Data Warehouse

   ```
   COPY INTO FactSales
   FROM 'lakehouse/sales_cleaned.parquet'
   WITH (FILE_TYPE = 'PARQUET');
   ```

   Best Practice: Use **Delta Lake format** for optimized querying.

   4.2. **Implementing Incremental Data Loads**

   Instead of loading the entire dataset, **incremental loads** improve performance.

   Example: Loading only new records using SQL

   ```
   INSERT INTO FactSales
   SELECT * FROM StagingSales
   WHERE SaleDate > (SELECT MAX(SaleDate) FROM FactSales);
   ```

   Best Practice: Use **Watermark Columns** (e.g., Last Modified Date) to track changes.

   4.3. **Optimizing Performance with Direct Lake Mode**

   Microsoft Fabric introduces **Direct Lake Mode**, allowing Power BI to directly query the lakehouse without importing data.

CHAPTER 3   IMPLEMENT A DATA WAREHOUSE WITH MICROSOFT FABRIC

Advantages

- No need for dataset refreshes
- Supports massive data volumes

Example: Enabling Direct Lake Mode in Power BI

- Connect Power BI to **Fabric Lakehouse**.
- Enable **Direct Lake connection**.

Best Practice: Use Direct Lake instead of Import Mode for real-time analytics.

5. **Automating the ETL Pipeline in Microsoft Fabric**

    5.1. **Orchestrating Workflows with Data Pipelines**

    Fabric's **Data Pipelines** automate data movement and transformation.

    Example: Creating a Data Pipeline

    1. **Extract**: Connect SQL Server, API, or Blob Storage.
    2. **Transform**: Use **Dataflows, Notebooks, or SQL Scripts**.
    3. **Load**: Store in **Lakehouse, Warehouse, or KQL Database**.
    4. **Schedule**: Set up **trigger-based or time-based** execution.

    5.2. **Using Event-Driven ETL with Real-Time Streaming**

    Fabric supports **real-time data ingestion** using **Event Streams and KQL databases**.

105

Use Case: Streaming IoT, logs, or social media data.

```
CREATE STREAMING TABLE RealTimeSales (
    SaleID INT,
    SaleAmount DECIMAL(10,2),
    SaleDate TIMESTAMP
);
```

6. **Security and Governance in ETL (DP-600 Key Points)**

   Implement Row-Level Security (RLS)

   Restrict user access based on roles.

   ```
   CREATE SECURITY POLICY SalesPolicy
   ADD FILTER PREDICATE UserRegion = 'East' ON FactSales;
   ```

   Data Masking for Sensitive Data

   Protect personal information.

   ```
   ALTER TABLE DimCustomers ALTER COLUMN PhoneNumber ADD MASKED WITH (FUNCTION = 'default()');
   ```

   Best Practice: Apply **security policies** for data governance.

7. **Best Practices for ETL in Microsoft Fabric (DP-600 Key Concepts)**

   Use ELT with Lakehouse for better scalability.

   Leverage Data Pipelines for workflow automation.

   Enable Direct Lake Mode for Power BI real-time analytics.

Optimize transformations using Spark Notebooks and SQL.

Implement Incremental Loading to improve efficiency.

Use Materialized Views and Partitioning for better performance.

Ensure Data Security with RLS and Data Masking.

Managing Data Storage and Performance in Microsoft Fabric

Introduction
Efficiently managing data storage and optimizing performance are **critical aspects of data warehousing** in Microsoft Fabric. As datasets grow, **proper storage strategies, indexing, partitioning, and query optimization techniques** ensure high performance and cost-effectiveness.

This section covers key storage and performance concepts relevant to **DP-600: Microsoft Fabric Analytics Engineer Associate**, including

- **Data Storage Strategies**
- **Partitioning and Distribution**
- **Indexing for Query Performance**
- **Optimizing ETL Processes**
- **Query Performance Tuning**
- **Monitoring and Performance Metrics**

1. **Data Storage Strategies in Microsoft Fabric**

   Microsoft Fabric provides a **lakehouse architecture** that integrates **structured, semi-structured, and unstructured data** into a unified platform. The key storage components are

Storage Type	Description	Best For
OneLake	Unified storage layer for structured, semi-structured, and unstructured data.	Storing all types of data in Fabric.
Data Warehouses	Optimized for **structured data** with relational processing.	High-performance **OLAP workloads**.
Lakehouses	Combines **data lakes + data warehouses** using Delta tables.	Big data analytics and structured queries.
KQL Databases	Used for real-time telemetry and log data analysis.	Time-series and **log analytics**.

   Best Practices for Storage Management

   Use **OneLake** as a centralized data repository.

   Store **structured data in Data Warehouses** for high-performance querying.

   Store **semi-structured data in Lakehouses** with Delta tables for **schema evolution**.

   Use **compression and file formats like Parquet** to reduce storage footprint.

2. **Partitioning and Distribution in Microsoft Fabric**

   Partitioning and distribution are **key techniques** to **improve query performance and scalability**.

Partitioning

Partitioning divides large tables into **smaller, manageable chunks** based on a key column (e.g., Date, Region, Category).

Types of Partitioning in Fabric Data Warehouse:

- **Range Partitioning**: Divides data based on a range (e.g., OrderDate)
- **Hash Partitioning**: Distributes data across partitions based on a hash function (e.g., CustomerID)
- **List Partitioning**: Segments data based on categories (e.g., Region—North, South)

Example: Range Partitioning by Year

```
CREATE TABLE Sales (
    OrderID INT,
    OrderDate DATE,
    Amount DECIMAL(10,2)
)
PARTITION BY RANGE (OrderDate) (
    PARTITION Sales_2019 VALUES LESS THAN ('2020-01-01'),
    PARTITION Sales_2020 VALUES LESS THAN ('2021-01-01'),
    PARTITION Sales_2021 VALUES LESS THAN ('2022-01-01')
);
```

Partitioning Benefits

- **Speeds up queries** by scanning only relevant partitions
- Improves **data management and archival**
- Enhances **parallel query execution**

Distribution Strategies

Fabric distributes tables across **compute nodes** to parallelize query execution.

Types of Table Distribution

- **Round Robin**: Evenly distributes rows but can lead to data shuffling
- **Replicated**: Stores a **copy of small tables** on all nodes (best for lookups)
- **Hash Distributed**: Distributes based on a key column (best for large fact tables)

Example: Hash Distribution on CustomerID

```
CREATE TABLE Sales (
    OrderID INT,
    CustomerID INT,
    OrderDate DATE,
    Amount DECIMAL(10,2)
)
DISTRIBUTED BY HASH (CustomerID);
```

Best Practices for Distribution

- Use **hash distribution** for large fact tables.
- Use **replicated tables** for small lookup tables to reduce **join overhead**.
- Avoid **round-robin** for large datasets due to data movement issues.

3. **Indexing for Query Performance**

Indexes **speed up query execution** by providing efficient lookup mechanisms. Microsoft Fabric supports:

Types of Indexes in Fabric

- **Clustered Index**: Organizes table rows in a sorted structure
- **Non-Clustered Index**: Creates a separate structure for quick lookups
- **Columnstore Index**: Best for large tables used in analytical queries

Example: Creating a Columnstore Index for Performance Optimization

```
CREATE CLUSTERED COLUMNSTORE INDEX idx_Sales ON Sales;
```

Indexing Best Practices

- Use **Clustered Columnstore Indexes** for analytical workloads (**default for Fabric DW**).
- Use **Non-Clustered Indexes** for frequently queried columns (e.g., CustomerID).

- **Avoid excessive indexing**, as it can impact **ETL performance**.

4. **Optimizing ETL Processes in Microsoft Fabric**

ETL (Extract, Transform, Load) is a crucial process in Fabric, and optimizing it **improves performance and reduces costs**.

Optimized ETL Workflow in Fabric

Extract: Load data from **OneLake, Azure SQL, or external sources**.

Transform: Use **Dataflows, Notebooks, or Spark jobs** for data transformation.

Load: Store in a **Data Warehouse or Lakehouse Delta table. Example: Efficient ELT in Fabric using T-SQL**

```
-- Extract data from staging
INSERT INTO Sales_Fact
SELECT * FROM Sales_Staging
WHERE OrderDate > DATEADD(DAY, -7, GETDATE());

-- Update necessary records
UPDATE Sales_Fact
SET Amount = Staging.Amount
FROM Sales_Fact Fact
INNER JOIN Sales_Staging Staging ON Fact.OrderID = Staging.OrderID;
```

Best Practices for ETL Optimization

- Use **PolyBase or Dataflows** for efficient data extraction.

- Implement **incremental loading** instead of full refreshes.
- Use **bulk insert operations** to improve loading speed.

5. **Query Performance Tuning**

Optimizing SQL queries **reduces execution time** and **improves performance**.

Common Performance Optimization Techniques

Use Proper Joins: Prefer **inner joins** over outer joins for better performance.

Avoid SELECT: Fetch only the required columns.

Use Indexed Columns in WHERE Clauses: Improves filtering speed.

Leverage Materialized Views: Store precomputed results for faster querying.

Example: Using a Materialized View for Performance

```
CREATE MATERIALIZED VIEW SalesSummary AS
SELECT CustomerID, SUM(Amount) AS TotalSales
FROM Sales_Fact
GROUP BY CustomerID;
```

Performance Tuning Best Practices

- Use **Materialized Views** for repeated aggregations.
- Optimize **joins and indexing** for faster lookups.
- Use **Partition Pruning** to scan only relevant partitions.

CHAPTER 3   IMPLEMENT A DATA WAREHOUSE WITH MICROSOFT FABRIC

6. **Monitoring and Performance Metrics**

    Microsoft Fabric provides **monitoring tools** to analyze storage and performance.

    Key Monitoring Tools

    - **Azure Monitor**: Tracks resource utilization and query performance
    - **Query Execution Plans**: Identifies slow-running queries and suggests optimizations
    - **Data Warehouse Metrics**: Monitors storage usage and query execution time

    Example: Checking Query Performance in Fabric

    ```
    EXPLAIN ANALYZE
    SELECT * FROM Sales_Fact WHERE OrderDate >= '2024-01-01';
    ```

    Best Practices for Monitoring Performance

    - Regularly **analyze query execution plans**.
    - Set up **alerts for high resource consumption**.
    - Use **query history logs** to track performance over time.

Chapter Summary

- Fabric Data Warehouse uses **OneLake, Lakehouses, and Data Warehouses** for structured and unstructured data.

CHAPTER 3   IMPLEMENT A DATA WAREHOUSE WITH MICROSOFT FABRIC

- OneLake serves as a **unified storage layer** across Fabric.

- Fabric SQL Endpoints provide **T-SQL support** for querying data in warehouses and lakehouses.

- Seamless integration with **Power BI, Synapse, and Azure services**.

- Use **OneLake for centralized storage**, **Delta tables for efficiency**, and **optimized partitioning** for performance.

- **Star Schema** is simple and fast, while **Snowflake Schema** reduces redundancy.

- **Fact Tables** store measurable data, and **Dimension Tables** provide descriptive attributes.

- **SCD Type 1** overwrites old data, **SCD Type 2** keeps historical records, **SCD Type 3** stores previous and current values, **SCD Type 4** maintains history in a separate table, and **SCD Type 6** is a hybrid approach.

- **Surrogate Keys** (auto-generated IDs) improve performance over **Natural Keys** (real-world identifiers).

- Use **Star Schema for analytics**, **SCD Type 2 for historical tracking**, and **Surrogate Keys for efficient joins**.

- **ETL** transforms data before loading; **ELT** transforms data inside the warehouse.

- **Dataflows, Data Factory Pipelines, Notebooks, and Spark** enable data ingestion in Fabric.

- **T-SQL, Python, and Spark** are used for data transformation.
- **Incremental loading** improves efficiency, while **Bulk insert operations** optimize performance.
- Use **incremental data loading**, **avoid full refreshes**, and **optimize joins and indexing**.
- **OneLake serves as unified storage**, with **Data Warehouses for structured analytics** and **Lakehouses for semi-structured data**.
- **Partitioning strategies** include **Range Partitioning (by date, region, etc.)** and **Hash Distribution (by customer ID, product ID)**.
- **Indexing Strategies** involve **Clustered Columnstore Index (default for analytics)** and **Non-Clustered Index (for lookups)**.
- **Materialized Views** optimize query performance.
- Use **Query Execution Plans** to diagnose slow queries.
- **Azure Monitor** helps track performance, while **Fabric Query History** analyzes slow queries.
- Use **Delta tables for storage efficiency**, **partition pruning for performance**, and **monitor queries regularly**.
- Understand **OneLake, Data Warehouses, and Lakehouses** in Fabric.
- Implement **Star Schema, Fact/Dimension Tables, and SCDs** effectively.

CHAPTER 3   IMPLEMENT A DATA WAREHOUSE WITH MICROSOFT FABRIC

- Optimize **ETL workflows** with best extraction, transformation, and loading techniques.
- Apply **partitioning, indexing, and query tuning** best practices.
- Monitor **queries with Azure Monitor, Query Plans, and Data Warehouse Metrics**.
- Next steps include **Data Security and Governance in Microsoft Fabric**.

CHAPTER 4

Work with Semantic Models in Microsoft Fabric

Chapter Overview

In this chapter, readers will explore the fundamental concepts, design principles, and best practices for working with **semantic models** in **Microsoft Fabric**. These models provide a structured representation of data, making it easier for users to perform meaningful analysis without requiring in-depth knowledge of the underlying data sources.

The chapter begins with an introduction to **semantic models**, explaining their role in data analytics, how they simplify complex data relationships, and why they are essential for building scalable and user-friendly analytics solutions. Readers will learn about the key components of semantic models, including tables, relationships, hierarchies, measures, and calculated columns, and how these elements contribute to better data comprehension.

Next, the focus shifts to **designing and creating semantic models** in Microsoft Fabric. Readers will gain practical insights into defining model structures, importing data from various sources, and ensuring consistency and accuracy in the data model. The chapter will also highlight key modeling techniques such as normalization, denormalization, and the use of **DAX (Data Analysis Expressions)** to create meaningful calculations.

Once the model is built, **optimizing for performance** becomes crucial. This chapter will cover various performance tuning strategies, such as **aggregations, indexing, partitioning, and query optimization**, to ensure the model operates efficiently, even with large datasets. Readers will also learn about reducing query execution times and improving report performance through best practices in model design.

Finally, **best practices in managing semantic models** will be explored. This includes strategies for version control, governance, security, and collaboration. Readers will understand how to implement **role-based access control (RBAC), security filters, and data refresh scheduling** to maintain a secure and up-to-date model. The chapter will also discuss monitoring and maintaining models for long-term usability.

By the end of this chapter, readers will have a comprehensive understanding of how to **design, optimize, and manage semantic models** in **Microsoft Fabric**, enabling them to build scalable, high-performance data models that enhance business intelligence and decision-making.

Key Terms

- **Semantic Model**: A structured data model in Microsoft Fabric that organizes data into tables, relationships, and business logic for analysis.

- **Fact Table**: A table containing transactional data, typically numeric values used for analysis (e.g., sales, revenue).

- **Dimension Table**: A table containing descriptive attributes used to filter or group fact table data (e.g., customers, dates, products).

- **Data Modeling**: The process of designing a structured framework for organizing and storing data in a semantic model.

- **Relationships**: Connections between tables (one-to-many, many-to-one, etc.) that define how data is linked in a model.

- **DAX (Data Analysis Expressions)**: A formula language used in Power BI and Fabric to create custom calculations and aggregations in a semantic model.

- **Row-Level Security (RLS)**: A security feature that restricts access to data rows based on user roles, ensuring users only see relevant data.

- **Object-Level Security (OLS)**: A security mechanism that hides entire tables or columns from unauthorized users.

- **Performance Analyzer**: A Power BI tool used to diagnose and optimize report performance by analyzing queries and visuals.

- **High Cardinality**: A condition where a column has many unique values, which can slow down performance and increase model size.

- **Aggregation**: A technique used to summarize data (e.g., sum, average, count) to improve performance by reducing dataset size.

CHAPTER 4   WORK WITH SEMANTIC MODELS IN MICROSOFT FABRIC

- **Incremental Refresh**: A process that loads only new or changed data instead of refreshing the entire dataset, improving efficiency.

- **Calculated Column**: A column created using DAX that derives new values based on existing data in the model.

- **Measure**: A dynamic calculation in DAX that aggregates data based on user interactions in reports.

- **Data Compression**: A technique used to reduce model size and improve performance by minimizing storage space for data.

- **Partitioning**: Splitting a large dataset into smaller, manageable parts to improve refresh and query performance.

- **Hierarchy**: A structured arrangement of data fields (e.g., Year ➤ Quarter ➤ Month ➤ Day) that allows for drill-down analysis.

- **Star Schema**: A widely used data modeling approach where a central fact table is linked to multiple dimension tables.

- **Snowflake Schema**: A more normalized version of a star schema where dimension tables are split into multiple related tables.

- **Deployment Pipeline**: A feature in Microsoft Fabric used to manage and automate semantic model deployments across development, staging, and production environments.

- **Version Control**: The practice of tracking and managing changes in semantic models using tools like GitHub or Azure DevOps.

- **Data Governance**: Policies and standards that ensure data consistency, quality, security, and compliance in a semantic model.

- **Model Optimization**: Techniques used to improve query speed, reduce load time, and enhance overall model efficiency.

- **Query Folding**: The process where transformations are pushed back to the data source for improved efficiency.

- **DirectQuery Mode**: A connection mode that retrieves data directly from the source in real time without loading it into memory.

- **Import Mode**: A connection mode that loads data into the model for faster query performance.

- **Composite Model**: A hybrid approach combining DirectQuery and Import modes for flexibility in data storage and performance.

- **Lazy Evaluation**: A technique where DAX calculations are executed only when needed to optimize performance.

- **Auto Aggregations**: A Fabric feature that automatically creates aggregations to improve query speed.

- **Dataflows**: ETL pipelines used to transform and prepare data before loading it into a semantic model.

- **Refresh Policy**: A set of rules defining how often and when data refreshes occur in a semantic model.

- **Model Documentation**: The process of maintaining records of model structure, relationships, measures, and calculations for future reference.

- **Thin Report**: A Power BI report that connects to an existing semantic model without duplicating data.

- **Dataset Endorsement**: A feature that marks datasets as Promoted or Certified to guide users toward reliable models.

- **Sensitivity Labels**: Metadata tags applied to datasets to classify and protect sensitive information.

- **Usage Metrics**: Insights into how a semantic model is used, helping in performance tuning and governance.

- **Query Performance Insights**: A tool that helps analyze and optimize slow-running queries in Power BI.

- **Time Intelligence Functions**: DAX functions that simplify calculations related to dates, such as year-to-date and moving averages.

- **Model Size Optimization**: The process of reducing memory usage in a semantic model by removing redundant data and optimizing calculations.

- **Data Source Credentials**: Authentication details required to connect a semantic model to external data sources.

- **Model Ownership**: The responsibility assigned to specific users or teams for maintaining and managing a semantic model.

CHAPTER 4   WORK WITH SEMANTIC MODELS IN MICROSOFT FABRIC

Introduction to Semantic Models

Semantic models play a crucial role in Microsoft Fabric by providing a structured, business-friendly representation of data that simplifies analysis and reporting. Instead of requiring users to query raw tables from a database, semantic models present the data in an intuitive format, allowing users to derive insights efficiently.

What Is a Semantic Model?

A **semantic model** is an **abstraction layer** that sits on top of raw data sources, organizing information in a way that makes sense to business users. It defines how data is structured, related, and calculated, ensuring a seamless and user-friendly data exploration experience. By encapsulating business logic, relationships, and calculations, semantic models allow end users to analyze data without needing to understand the complexities of database schema or SQL queries. Refer to Figure 4-1.

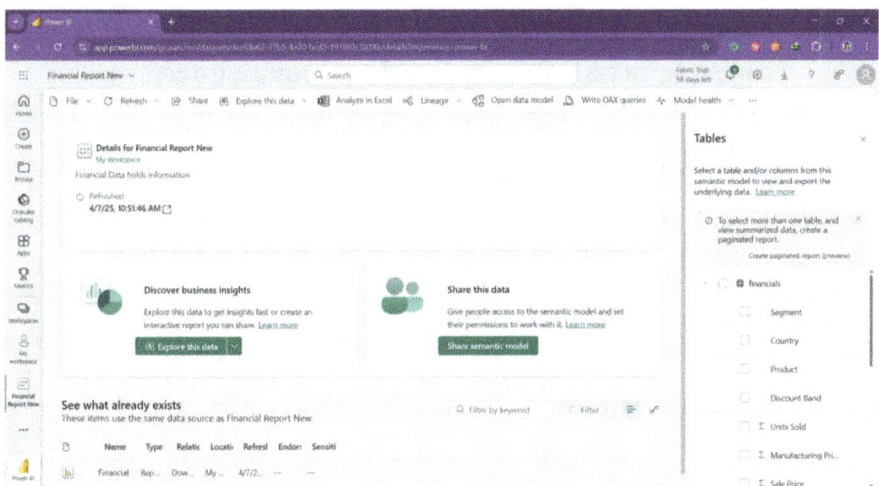

Figure 4-1. *Semantic model in Microsoft Fabric Power BI*

Why Are Semantic Models Important?

1. **Simplifies Data Access**: Instead of dealing with raw database tables, users interact with well-structured, labeled entities such as "Sales," "Customers," or "Products."

2. **Improves Performance**: Predefined aggregations, relationships, and calculations reduce query execution time, enhancing efficiency.

3. **Encapsulates Business Logic**: Measures, calculated columns, and hierarchies ensure that reports and dashboards follow standardized business rules.

4. **Enhances Data Security**: Row-level security (RLS) and role-based access control (RBAC) ensure that users see only the data relevant to them.

5. **Supports Self-Service Analytics**: Business users can perform ad hoc analysis without requiring deep technical knowledge of SQL or database structures.

Key Components of a Semantic Model

A well-structured semantic model consists of several essential components that help in defining relationships, calculations, and data access:

1. **Tables and Columns**: Represent structured data from different sources as shown in Figure 4-2 (e.g., Sales table with Date, Amount, and Product fields).

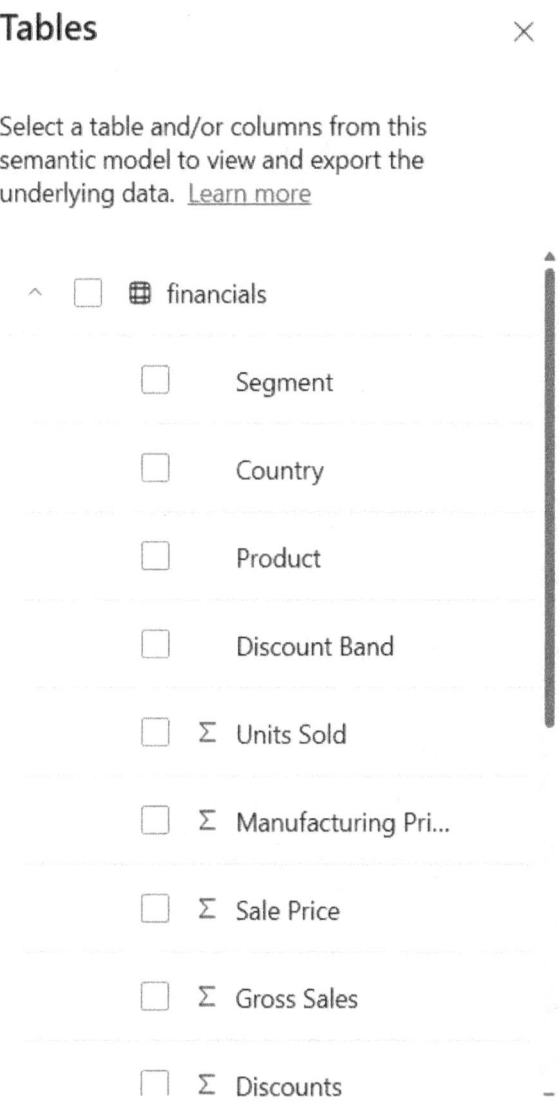

Figure 4-2. *Tables and columns in semantic model*

CHAPTER 4   WORK WITH SEMANTIC MODELS IN MICROSOFT FABRIC

2. **Relationships**: Define how tables are linked using keys as shown in Figure 4-3 (e.g., a relationship between Orders and Customers based on CustomerID).

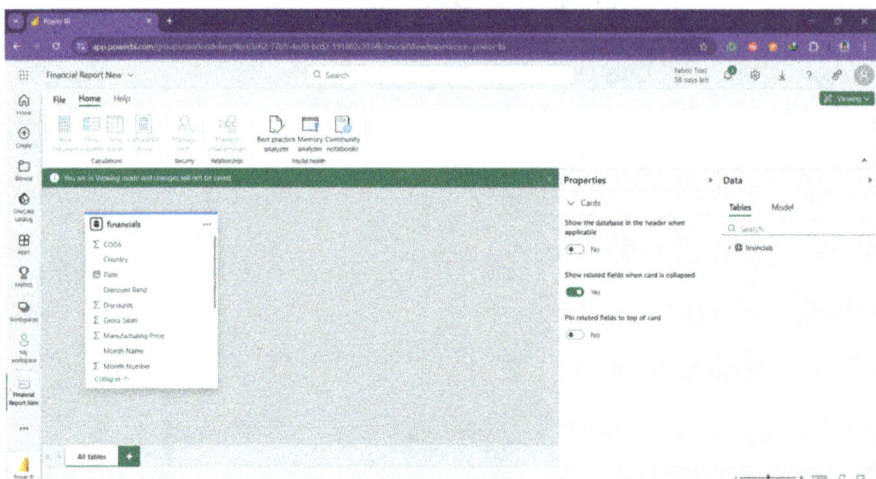

Figure 4-3. *Data model (relationship)*

3. **Measures and Calculations**: Created using **DAX (Data Analysis Expressions)** to perform aggregations like **Total Sales, Average Revenue, or Year-over-Year Growth as shown in Figure 4-4.**

CHAPTER 4 WORK WITH SEMANTIC MODELS IN MICROSOFT FABRIC

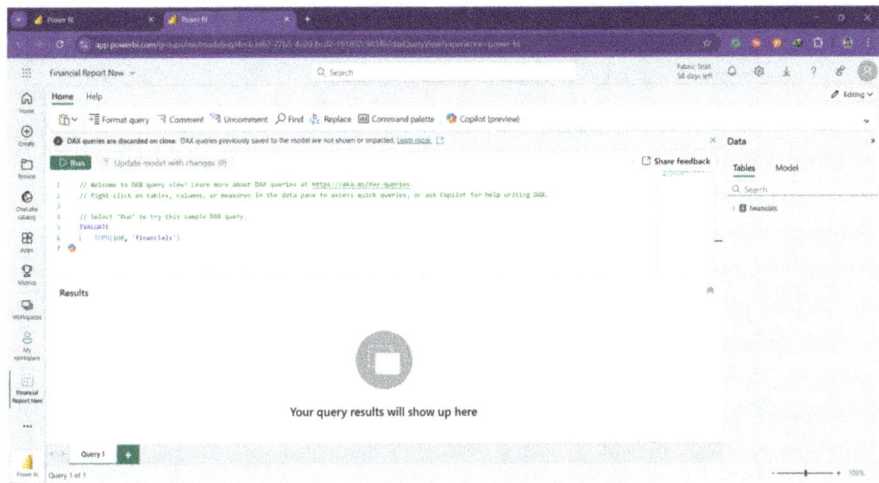

Figure 4-4. DAX view

4. **Hierarchies**: Enable drill-down functionality in reports (e.g., a hierarchy for Year ➤ Quarter ➤ Month ➤ Day).

5. **Security Rules**: Implement Row-Level Security (RLS) and Object-Level Security (OLS) to control access to sensitive data. Refer to Figure 4-5's screenshot to share your semantic model.

CHAPTER 4   WORK WITH SEMANTIC MODELS IN MICROSOFT FABRIC

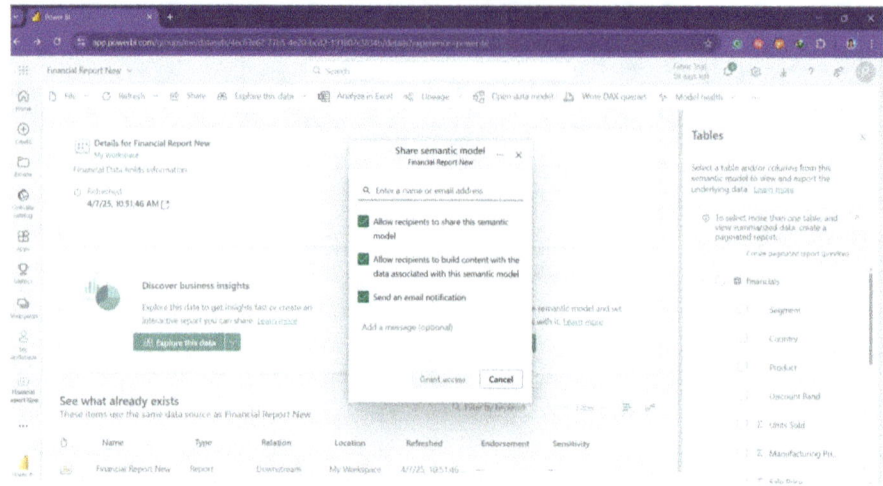

Figure 4-5. *Sharing the semantic model*

6. **Data Refresh and Storage Mode**: Defines whether the data is **imported, direct query-based, or hybrid (composite models)** for real-time or scheduled updates.

How Semantic Models Work in Microsoft Fabric

In **Microsoft Fabric**, semantic models integrate seamlessly with **Power BI, Data Warehouse, and Lakehouse** environments. Users can create models based on **OneLake**, **Azure SQL Database**, **Synapse Analytics**, or other sources, enabling unified data exploration.

1. **Data Connection**: Fabric allows users to connect to various data sources, including structured (SQL, Excel) and unstructured (Lakehouse, Delta tables) datasets.

2. **Data Modeling**: Users design relationships between tables, create calculations with DAX, and define hierarchies.

3. **Performance Optimization**: Features like aggregations, indexing, and caching improve query performance.

4. **Consumption and Analysis**: The model is used in Power BI reports, dashboards, or external applications via APIs.

Real-World Use Cases of Semantic Models

- **Finance and Accounting:** Creating a revenue analysis model that enables business analysts to drill down from yearly profits to individual transactions.

- **Retail and E-Commerce:** A product sales model linking data across customers, transactions, and inventory to generate insights on top-selling products.

- **Healthcare and Research:** A patient data model integrating multiple sources (EHR, lab results) for better decision-making.

- **Manufacturing and Supply Chain:** A logistics model analyzing supplier performance, order delays, and stock levels across warehouses.

Designing and Creating Semantic Models

Designing and creating a **semantic model** in **Microsoft Fabric** is a critical step in enabling efficient data analysis. A well-structured semantic model ensures that users can interact with data intuitively while maintaining **accuracy, performance, and scalability**. This section provides a comprehensive guide on the **design principles, model creation process, and key best practices** to build effective semantic models in Microsoft Fabric.

Understanding the Design of a Semantic Model

Before building a semantic model, it is essential to **understand business requirements**, data sources, and performance considerations. The goal is to **transform raw data into a structured, business-friendly model** that enhances reporting and analytics.

Key considerations in designing a semantic model include

1. **Business Understanding**: Identify key metrics, relationships, and hierarchies relevant to business users.

2. **Data Source Selection**: Choose appropriate sources such as OneLake, Azure SQL, Synapse, Data Warehouse, or Lakehouse tables.

3. **Data Structure Design**: Plan tables, relationships, and aggregations to optimize performance.

4. **Scalability and Performance**: Implement best practices for handling large datasets efficiently.

Steps to Create a Semantic Model in Microsoft Fabric

1. **Connect to Data Sources**

   The first step in creating a semantic model is establishing a connection with **structured or unstructured data sources** in Microsoft Fabric. Common sources include

   - **OneLake Tables**: Unified storage for structured and semi-structured data

   - **Azure SQL Database/Synapse Analytics**: Relational data sources for enterprise solutions

CHAPTER 4   WORK WITH SEMANTIC MODELS IN MICROSOFT FABRIC

- **Data Warehouse and Lakehouse**: Scalable data storage options integrated with Fabric
- **Excel/CSV/APIs**: External sources used for supplementary data

In **Microsoft Fabric**, users can import data using **Power BI Dataflows**, DirectQuery, or Composite Models for flexible data access.

2. **Define Tables and Data Structure**

   Once the data is connected, the next step is defining tables and organizing data efficiently.

   - **Fact Tables**: Contain transactional or event-based data (e.g., Sales, Orders, Transactions).
   - **Dimension Tables**: Contain descriptive attributes (e.g., Customers, Products, Dates).
   - **Star vs. Snowflake Schema**: Select an appropriate schema for performance optimization.

   Example: Sales Data Model Structure

Table Name	Type	Key Columns	Description
Sales	Fact	SaleID, DateID, ProductID	Contains sales transactions.
Customers	Dimension	CustomerID	Stores customer details.
Products	Dimension	ProductID	Holds product information.
Date	Dimension	DateID	Provides date-related attributes.

3. **Establish Relationships Between Tables**

   Relationships define how tables interact within the model. In Fabric, relationships can be **one-to-many (1:M), one-to-one (1:1), or many-to-many (M:M)**.

   - **Primary Key (PK)–Foreign Key (FK) Relationships**: Connect fact and dimension tables.
   - **Active vs. Inactive Relationships**: Define how tables interact for reporting.
   - **Bidirectional vs. Single Direction Filtering**: Control how filters propagate across tables.

   Example Relationship: Sales and Customers

   - **Sales** (Fact) → **Customers** (Dimension) using CustomerID.
   - **Sales** (Fact) → **Products** (Dimension) using ProductID.

   Microsoft Fabric allows **visual relationship modeling** in Power BI and Fabric environments, simplifying model creation.

4. **Create Measures and Calculations Using DAX**

   Measures and calculations **add analytical power** to semantic models. Microsoft Fabric supports **DAX (Data Analysis Expressions)** to define custom metrics.

   Common DAX Measures

   - **Total Sales**: Total Sales = SUM(Sales[Amount])

- **Average Order Value**: AOV = DIVIDE([Total Sales], COUNT(Sales[SaleID]))

- **Year-over-Year Growth**: YoY Growth = ([Total Sales] - [Total Sales LY]) / [Total Sales LY]

DAX measures help create **dynamic calculations**, improving the model's analytical capabilities.

5. **Implement Hierarchies for Drill-Down Analysis**

    Hierarchies allow users to **navigate data at different levels of granularity** in reports.
    Example Hierarchies

    - **Date Hierarchy:** Year → Quarter → Month → Day
    - **Geographical Hierarchy:** Country → State → City
    - **Product Hierarchy:** Category → Subcategory → Product

    Hierarchies improve the **user experience** in Power BI reports, enabling drill-down functionality.

6. **Configure Data Refresh and Storage Mode**

    Microsoft Fabric supports different storage modes for performance optimization:

    - **Import Mode:** Data is loaded into memory for fast performance.
    - **DirectQuery Mode:** Queries data directly from the source in real time.
    - **Composite Models:** A hybrid approach combining Import and DirectQuery.

    Selecting the right mode depends on **data size, refresh frequency, and latency requirements.**

7. **Implement Security and Role-Based Access Control (RBAC)**

   Ensuring **data security and governance** is crucial when designing a semantic model. Microsoft Fabric provides

   - **Row-Level Security (RLS)**: Restricts data access based on user roles
   - **Object-Level Security (OLS)**: Hides entire tables or columns based on permissions
   - **Workspace Permissions**: Controls model access in **Microsoft Fabric and Power BI**

   Example: RLS Implementation

```
SalesSecurity = FILTER(Sales, Sales[Region] = USERPRINCIPALNAME())
```

This ensures users can only view sales data for their assigned region.

Best Practices for Designing Semantic Models

To build an optimized and scalable model, follow these best practices:

1. **Use Star Schema**: Reduce complexity and improve query performance.
2. **Optimize Relationships**: Use single-direction filtering for better performance.
3. **Minimize Calculated Columns**: Prefer measures over calculated columns for efficiency.
4. **Implement Aggregations**: Store pre-calculated summaries to speed up queries.
5. **Partition Large Tables**: Improve query performance for massive datasets.

6. **Use Proper Data Types**: Avoid unnecessary conversions for faster processing.

7. **Regularly Monitor and Optimize**: Review model performance using **Performance Analyzer** in Power BI.

Optimizing Semantic Models for Performance

Optimizing a **semantic model** is critical to ensuring fast query execution, efficient data handling, and scalability, especially in **Microsoft Fabric** environments where large datasets are processed. A poorly optimized model can result in **slow reports, inefficient queries, and resource bottlenecks.** This section provides a detailed guide on how to **enhance the performance** of semantic models by leveraging best practices, storage optimizations, and advanced techniques.

Understanding Performance Optimization in Semantic Models

Performance optimization in **Microsoft Fabric** revolves around

1. **Data Model Design**: Structuring tables, relationships, and schemas efficiently

2. **Query Performance**: Ensuring DAX calculations and queries execute quickly

3. **Storage Mode Optimization**: Choosing between **Import, DirectQuery, or Composite Mode**

4. **Data Refresh Optimization**: Reducing refresh time and improving data load performance

5. **Security and Indexing**: Implementing Row-Level Security (RLS) efficiently without slowing down queries

Each of these factors impacts the **speed, responsiveness, and scalability** of the semantic model in **Power BI and Microsoft Fabric** environments.

1. **Optimize Data Model Design**

   The **data model structure** plays a crucial role in query performance. A well-designed model minimizes redundant calculations and ensures efficient data retrieval.

   a) **Use a Star Schema Instead of a Snowflake Schema**

   - **Star Schema** (Recommended): Uses a **single fact table** connected to multiple **dimension tables**, reducing query complexity
   - **Snowflake Schema**: Normalizes dimension tables into sub-tables, increasing the number of joins, which **slows down performance**

   Example: Instead of breaking the **Customer** table into multiple sub-tables (e.g., Customer Details, Customer Address, Customer Contact), keep it **denormalize0d in a single dimension table.**

   b) **Reduce the Number of Active Relationships**

   - **Use single-direction relationships where possible** (instead of bidirectional).
   - **Minimize unnecessary relationships**: Each relationship requires processing power.
   - **Use inactive relationships if required**: Activate them only in specific DAX calculations using USERELATIONSHIP().

c) **Avoid Using Too Many Calculated Columns**

- Instead of **creating calculated columns in the model**, prefer **DAX measures**, as they are computed only when needed.

- If a calculated column is required, **consider pre-calculating it in the data source** to reduce computation overhead.

Example

Use a measure instead of a calculated column:

`Total Sales = SUM(Sales[Amount])`

Avoid calculated columns that replicate existing measures:

`SalesAmount = Sales[Quantity] * Sales[UnitPrice]`

// This should be done in the source, not in the model

2. **Optimize Query Performance in DAX**

Poorly written **DAX queries** can slow down report performance. Follow these **best practices** to improve execution speed:

a) **Use Aggregations Instead of Row-Level Calculations**

- Pre-aggregate data to avoid **row-by-row computations**.

- Use SUMX() carefully, as it iterates over rows and can be **resource-intensive**.

Optimized Aggregation Using Measures:

`Total Sales = SUM(Sales[Amount])`

Avoid Row-by-Row Computation:

```
Total Sales = SUMX(Sales, Sales[Quantity] * Sales[Unit Price])
```

b) **Reduce Cardinality of Columns**

- **Cardinality** refers to the number of unique values in a column.
- High-cardinality columns slow down calculations.
- Avoid storing unnecessary **IDs, timestamps, or high-granularity data**.

Example

Convert High-Cardinality Columns to Categorical Data

Instead of storing **exact timestamps (e.g., "2025-03-17 12:34:56")**, store **date-only values (e.g., "2025-03-17")** and create a separate **Time Dimension Table**.

3. **Optimize Storage Mode for Performance**

Microsoft Fabric offers three storage modes:

1. **Import Mode** (Fastest): Data is loaded into memory (cache).
2. **DirectQuery Mode** (Real Time): Queries live data from the source (slower performance).
3. **Composite Mode**: A mix of Import and DirectQuery.

Best Practices for Storage Mode Selection

- **Use Import Mode When Possible**: Best for fast performance with smaller datasets.

- **Use DirectQuery Only for Real-Time Data Needs**: Avoid if the source is slow.

- **Use Aggregations in Composite Models**: Store summary data in Import Mode and detailed data in DirectQuery.

Example: Using Aggregations in Composite Models

- Store **daily total sales in Import Mode**.
- Store **transaction-level data in DirectQuery Mode**.
- Queries at the **summary level** will run faster, while detailed queries will fetch real-time data.

4. **Optimize Data Refresh Performance**

If a **semantic model** takes too long to refresh, it can impact performance.

Best Practices for Faster Data Refresh

- **Incremental Refresh**: Instead of reloading the entire dataset, refresh only **new or updated data**.

- **Partition Large Tables**: Split data into smaller partitions (e.g., by month or year).

- **Avoid Complex Transformations in Power Query**: Perform data cleaning at the source level (SQL, Data Warehouse) instead.

Example: Implementing Incremental Refresh for Sales Data

RangeStart = DATE(2024,1,1)
RangeEnd = DATE(2024,12,31)

- Only refresh data **from the last 6 months**, reducing refresh time significantly.

5. **Optimize Security and Role-Level Filtering**

   Row-Level Security (RLS) can impact performance **if not optimized**.

   Best Practices for RLS Optimization

   - **Filter at the Fact Table level, NOT the Dimension Table level.**
   - **Avoid Using Dynamic Security with USERPRINCIPALNAME() unless necessary.**
   - **Pre-filter data at the source if possible.**

   Optimized RLS Implementation

   SalesSecurity = FILTER(Sales, Sales[Region] = USERPRINCIPALNAME())

   - Applies **direct filtering** at the fact table level, reducing query complexity

   Optimizing semantic models in **Microsoft Fabric** ensures efficient data handling, faster reports, and scalable analytics. By following best practices such as

   - **Using a Star Schema** instead of a Snowflake Schema
   - **Optimizing DAX measures**
   - **Reducing cardinality**
   - **Choosing the right storage mode**
   - **Implementing 6incremental refresh**

you can **significantly improve performance**.

The next section will cover **Best Practices in Model Management**, ensuring long-term efficiency and maintainability of semantic models in **Microsoft Fabric**.

Best Practices in Model Management

Effective **model management** ensures that your **semantic models in Microsoft Fabric** remain efficient, scalable, and maintainable over time. Poorly managed models can lead to **performance degradation, security vulnerabilities, and increased complexity**. This section outlines the **best practices** for managing semantic models, covering areas such as **model governance, documentation, version control, security, collaboration, and life cycle management**.

1. **Implement a Structured Model Governance Strategy**

    Model governance refers to the structured process of managing, monitoring, and maintaining semantic models to ensure **data consistency, security, and performance**.

    Key Principles of Governance

    - **Define Naming Conventions**: Use a clear and consistent naming pattern for tables, columns, and measures.
        - Example: Use SalesAmount instead of Sales_amt1 or amt.
    - **Enforce Data Model Documentation**: Keep detailed documentation on data sources, relationships, measures, and security roles.
    - **Standardize Business Logic**: Define **consistent DAX calculations and KPIs** to avoid discrepancies in different reports.

Example of Naming Convention Guidelines

- **Fact Tables**: Fact_Sales, Fact_Orders
- **Dimension Tables**: Dim_Customer, Dim_Date
- **Measures**: Total Sales, Average Revenue

2. **Version Control and Change Management**

   Maintaining **version control** prevents data inconsistencies and helps teams track changes efficiently.

   ### Best Practices for Version Control

   - Use **source control repositories** (e.g., GitHub, Azure DevOps) to manage model changes.
   - Implement **a change log** to document updates, modifications, and fixes.
   - **Test changes in a development environment** before deploying them in production.
   - Use **deployment pipelines** in Microsoft Fabric to automate version management and model promotion.

   ### Example of a Change Log Entry

Date	Change Description	Author	Version
2025-03-15	Added 'Total Profit' measure	John Doe	v1.1
2025-03-20	Optimized 'Sales Performance' DAX	Jane Smith	v1.2

3. **Optimize Security and Access Control**

   Security plays a critical role in model management, ensuring that only authorized users access sensitive data.

   Best Practices for Security

   - Implement **Row-Level Security (RLS)** to restrict data access based on user roles.
   - Use **Object-Level Security (OLS)** to hide entire tables or columns from unauthorized users.
   - **Use Microsoft Entra ID (Azure AD)** for user authentication and group-based permissions.

   Example of Row-Level Security in DAX:

   ```
   SalesSecurity = FILTER(Sales, Sales[Region] = USERPRINCIPALNAME())
   ```

   - Ensures that users only see data relevant to their **assigned region**

4. **Maintain Data Quality and Consistency**

   Poor data quality can lead to inaccurate insights and flawed decision-making.

   Best Practices for Data Quality

   - **Monitor Data Refresh Failures**: Use Microsoft Fabric monitoring tools to track refresh errors.
   - **Standardize Data Formats**: Ensure uniform **date formats, currency symbols, and numerical precision** across all datasets.
   - **Deduplicate Data**: Remove redundant records before loading them into the model.

- **Perform Regular Data Validation**: Compare model outputs with source data to identify inconsistencies.

Example

- Convert **MM/DD/YYYY** format to **YYYY-MM-DD** to maintain consistency across reports.

5. **Optimize Model Performance with Regular Maintenance**

   Even well-built models require periodic performance tuning to prevent slow queries and refresh bottlenecks.

   Best Practices for Model Optimization

   - **Monitor Performance Metrics**: Use **Performance Analyzer** in Power BI to identify slow DAX queries.
   - **Remove Unused Columns and Tables**: Keep only the necessary fields to reduce model size.
   - **Implement Incremental Refresh**: Reduce data refresh time by loading only new data.
   - **Optimize Relationships and Cardinality**: Avoid high-cardinality columns that slow down calculations.

   Example of Performance Analyzer Output (Identifying Slow Queries)

Query Name	Execution Time (ms)	Optimization Required?
Sales by Region	4500 ms	☑ Yes – Rewrite DAX
Customer Segmentation	300 ms	✗ No

6. **Establish Collaboration and Documentation Standards**

   Clear documentation and collaboration guidelines ensure that multiple users can work on the model efficiently.

   Best Practices for Collaboration

   - **Use Microsoft OneDrive, SharePoint, or Teams** for shared model documentation.

   - **Enable Co-Authoring in Power BI Service**: Allow multiple contributors to update models.

   - **Use Data Cataloging Tools**: Leverage **Microsoft Purview** to catalog data assets and their usage.

   Example of a Documentation Template

Component	Description	Owner	Last Updated
Fact_Sales	Sales transaction data	John Doe	2025-03-10
Dim_Customer	Customer demographic details	Jane Smith	2025-03-15

7. **Implement Life Cycle Management for Semantic Models**

   Semantic models go through different stages of development, deployment, and retirement. Managing this life cycle ensures efficiency.

   Best Practices for Life Cycle Management

   - **Follow a Three-Tier Environment:**
     - **Development**: Testing new features

- **Staging**: Validating before production deployment
- **Production**: Finalized model used for reporting
- **Schedule Regular Model Reviews**: Identify performance or security issues proactively.
- **Decommission Unused Models**: Remove old or redundant models to optimize resource usage.

Example of a Model Life Cycle

1. **Version 1.0:** Initial model deployment
2. **Version 1.1:** Added new measures for sales performance
3. **Version 1.2:** Optimized refresh strategy and security roles
4. **Version 1.3:** Model retired and replaced with a new structure

Managing **semantic models in Microsoft Fabric** requires a structured approach to governance, security, performance optimization, and life cycle management. By following these best practices, you can ensure that your models remain **efficient, scalable, and easy to maintain**, ultimately supporting **high-quality data analysis and business intelligence workflows**.

With effective **model management**, you can

- Ensure **consistent data governance** across teams.
- Improve **model performance** and reduce refresh times.
- Maintain **security and compliance** with access control.
- Enable **collaboration** and seamless **version tracking**.

Chapter Summary

- Semantic models in Microsoft Fabric provide a structured approach to organizing, managing, and analyzing data.

- These models help bridge the gap between raw data and meaningful business insights by defining relationships, measures, and hierarchies.

- Creating a well-designed semantic model involves identifying fact and dimension tables, setting up relationships, and ensuring data integrity.

- Proper optimization techniques, such as aggregations, indexing, partitioning, and query folding, improve performance and scalability.

- Implementing security features like Row-Level Security (RLS) and Object-Level Security (OLS) ensures data access is restricted based on user roles.

- Best practices in model management, including version control, documentation, refresh scheduling, and governance policies, help maintain efficiency and reliability.

- The use of DAX (Data Analysis Expressions) enables advanced calculations and custom aggregations within the model.

- Different storage modes (Import, DirectQuery, and Composite) provide flexibility in handling large datasets while balancing performance and real-time access.

- Deployment pipelines streamline the process of moving semantic models across development, testing, and production environments.

- Understanding and applying optimization techniques, including reducing model size, using efficient data types, and leveraging performance analyzer tools, enhances user experience.

- Proper data governance ensures data consistency, quality, and compliance with organizational and regulatory requirements.

- Microsoft Fabric's integration with Power BI and other analytics tools enables seamless reporting and interactive data exploration.

- The continuous monitoring of model usage, performance, and refresh metrics helps in proactive tuning and long-term maintenance.

CHAPTER 5

Administer and Govern Microsoft Fabric

Chapter Overview

Effective administration and governance are critical for ensuring the security, compliance, and performance of Microsoft Fabric. This chapter provides a comprehensive guide to managing users, securing data, monitoring system performance, and implementing governance best practices.

We begin by exploring **User and Access Management**, covering how to configure role-based access control (RBAC), manage permissions, and integrate with Microsoft Entra ID (formerly Azure AD) to maintain secure authentication and authorization.

Next, we delve into **Data Security and Compliance**, addressing essential security measures such as encryption, data loss prevention (DLP), sensitivity labels, and regulatory compliance frameworks like GDPR and HIPAA.

The chapter then shifts focus to **Monitoring and Performance Optimization**, where we discuss tools and strategies for tracking system health, auditing activities, troubleshooting performance bottlenecks, and optimizing resources to ensure efficient Fabric workloads.

CHAPTER 5   ADMINISTER AND GOVERN MICROSOFT FABRIC

Finally, we outline **Governance Best Practices**, including setting up policies, enforcing data stewardship, managing workspaces effectively, and ensuring compliance with organizational standards.

By the end of this chapter, you will have a strong understanding of how to administer and govern Microsoft Fabric effectively, enabling secure and scalable data operations.

Key Terms

- **Role-Based Access Control (RBAC)**: A security model that assigns permissions based on user roles to enforce least privilege access.

- **Policy-Based Access Control (PBAC)**: A dynamic access control model that grants permissions based on attributes like data classification, location, or device.

- **Multi-Factor Authentication (MFA)**: An additional security layer requiring users to verify their identity using multiple authentication methods.

- **Row-Level Security (RLS)**: A security feature that restricts access to specific rows of data within a dataset based on user identity.

- **Microsoft Entra ID (Formerly Azure Active Directory)**: A cloud-based identity and access management service used for authentication and user management.

- **Microsoft Purview**: A governance and compliance tool that provides data discovery, classification, and protection features.

- **Data Classification**: The process of categorizing data based on sensitivity levels such as Public, Internal, Confidential, or Restricted.

- **Sensitivity Labels**: Metadata tags applied to datasets to enforce security policies like encryption, access restrictions, or compliance controls.

- **Data Encryption**: A security measure that encodes data to protect it from unauthorized access, using technologies like AES-256 encryption.

- **Data Loss Prevention (DLP)**: Policies and controls that prevent unauthorized sharing or leakage of sensitive data.

- **Compliance Standards (GDPR, HIPAA, ISO 27001)**: Regulatory frameworks that govern data privacy, security, and compliance requirements.

- **Audit Logging**: The process of recording user activities, data access, and modifications for security and compliance tracking.

- **Data Lineage**: A tracking mechanism that provides visibility into data origins, transformations, and usage within Microsoft Fabric.

- **Microsoft Defender for Cloud**: A cloud security tool that helps detect threats and vulnerabilities within Microsoft Fabric environments.

- **Azure Monitor**: A monitoring service that provides insights into system performance, resource utilization, and operational health.

CHAPTER 5   ADMINISTER AND GOVERN MICROSOFT FABRIC

- **Workload Management**: The process of optimizing system resources and query execution for improved performance in Microsoft Fabric.

- **Resource Optimization**: Techniques such as auto-scaling, caching, and indexing to enhance system efficiency and reduce costs.

- **Governance Framework**: A structured set of policies, roles, and processes that ensure secure and compliant data management.

- **Data Stewardship**: The responsibility of managing and maintaining data quality, security, and compliance within an organization.

- **Data Retention Policies**: Rules that define how long data should be stored and when it should be archived or deleted.

- **Access Audits**: Regular reviews of user permissions and access controls to ensure security best practices are followed.

- **Automated Governance**: The use of AI and automation tools to enforce security policies, detect anomalies, and streamline governance processes.

- **Proactive Issue Resolution**: A strategy that involves real-time monitoring and alerts to detect and mitigate potential performance or security issues before they impact users.

User and Access Management in Microsoft Fabric

Effective user and access management is essential for ensuring data security, compliance, and smooth collaboration within Microsoft Fabric. This section provides a detailed guide on managing users, assigning roles, configuring permissions, and integrating identity providers.

1. **Identity and Authentication in Microsoft Fabric**

    1.1. **Microsoft Entra ID (Azure Active Directory) Integration**

    Microsoft Fabric relies on **Microsoft Entra ID (formerly Azure Active Directory)** for authentication and identity management. Key features include

    - **Single Sign-On (SSO)**: Allows users to access Fabric services using their organizational credentials
    - **Multi-Factor Authentication (MFA)**: Enhances security by requiring an additional verification step
    - **Conditional Access Policies**: Controls access based on user identity, device security status, and location
    - **Federation with External Identity Providers**: Supports Google, Facebook, and third-party SAML-based authentication

1.2. **Authentication Methods**

Fabric supports various authentication methods:

- **Password-Based Authentication**: Traditional username-password login.

- **Certificate-Based Authentication**: Uses digital certificates for secure logins.

- **Token-Based Authentication**: OAuth and OpenID Connect (OIDC) for seamless authentication with apps and services.

- **Managed Identities**: Securely authenticate applications without storing credentials.

2. **User Roles and Permissions in Microsoft Fabric**

   2.1. **Role-Based Access Control (RBAC)**

   Microsoft Fabric uses **RBAC** to manage permissions effectively. The steps are shown through Figures 5-1 and 5-2. Table 5-1 shows the key roles.

CHAPTER 5   ADMINISTER AND GOVERN MICROSOFT FABRIC

Table 5-1. *Roles in Microsoft Fabric*

Role	Description
Admin	Full control over Microsoft Fabric, including settings, security, and monitoring.
Capacity Admin	Manages capacity settings, assigns workspaces, and monitors resource usage.
Workspace Admin	Controls workspace settings, assigns roles, and manages content.
Member	Can create and modify content within a workspace but cannot manage workspace settings.
Contributor	Can edit datasets and reports but cannot delete content or change permissions.
Viewer	Read-only access to reports and dashboards.

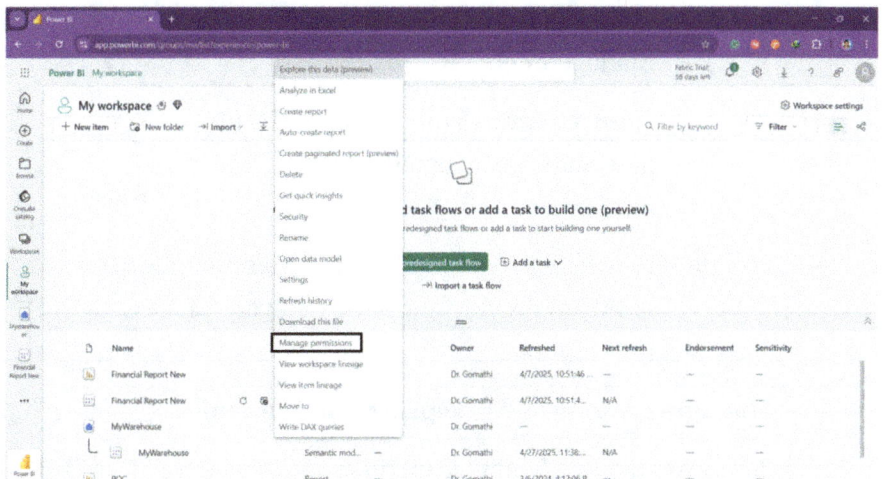

Figure 5-1. *Manage permissions*

CHAPTER 5   ADMINISTER AND GOVERN MICROSOFT FABRIC

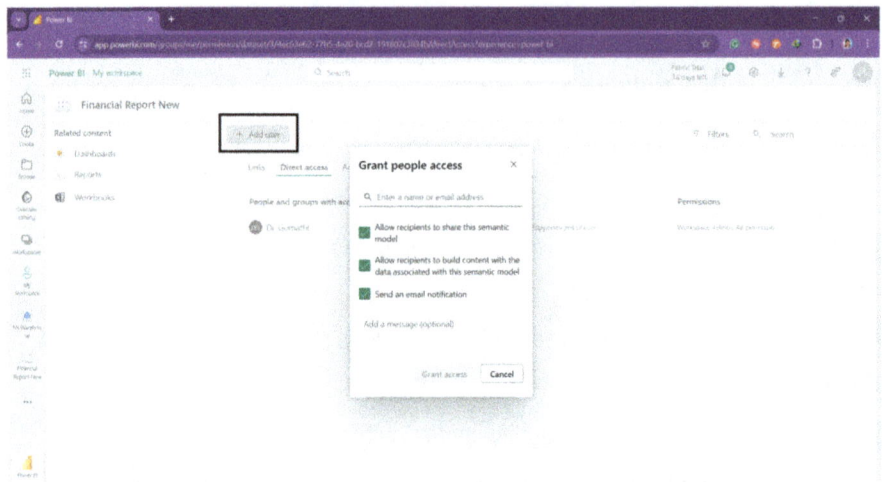

Figure 5-2. *Click Add user—you will get a small window to grant the user access.*

   2.2. **Assigning Users and Groups to Roles**

   - Assign **individual users** or **Microsoft Entra ID groups** to roles to streamline access management.

   - Use **Dynamic Groups** in Entra ID to automatically assign users based on attributes.

   - Leverage **Privileged Identity Management (PIM)** to provide temporary elevated access for admins.

3. **Managing Access to Workspaces and Content**

   3.1. **Workspace Access Control**

   Each workspace in Microsoft Fabric can have **specific access levels**:

- **Admin**: Full control over the workspace, including adding/removing users.
- **Member**: Can edit reports and datasets but cannot manage users.
- **Contributor**: Can modify content but not delete or manage workspace settings.
- **Viewer**: Can only view reports and datasets.

Admins can **restrict sharing settings** to prevent unauthorized access or accidental data leaks.

3.2. Sharing and Permissions for Reports and Dashboards

- **Direct Sharing**: Share reports via links or email invitations.
- **Row-Level Security (RLS)**: Restrict data access within a dataset based on user roles.
- **Sensitivity Labels**: Classify content with labels like "Confidential" or "Public" to enforce security policies.
- **Data Loss Prevention (DLP) Policies**: Prevent sharing of sensitive information externally.

3.3. External User Access (B2B Collaboration)

Microsoft Fabric supports **external user collaboration** via Microsoft Entra ID B2B:

- **Guest users** can be added to workspaces with restricted permissions.

- **Azure AD B2B Collaboration** allows secure sharing with partners, vendors, and customers.

- **Conditional Access Policies** ensure external users meet security requirements before accessing data.

4. **Automating User and Access Management**

    4.1. **Using Microsoft Entra ID Groups for Automation**

    - **Dynamic Groups**: Automatically add users based on attributes (e.g., department, location).

    - **Security Groups**: Assign permissions to groups rather than individual users for easier management.

    - **Distribution Lists**: Simplify communication with multiple users at once.

    4.2. **Power Automate for Access Management**

    - **Automate user onboarding** by assigning new employees to appropriate Fabric workspaces.

    - **Trigger access revocation** when an employee leaves or moves departments.

    - **Monitor permissions** and receive alerts when unauthorized access changes occur.

    4.3. **API-Based Access Control**

    Microsoft Fabric offers APIs to programmatically manage access:

CHAPTER 5   ADMINISTER AND GOVERN MICROSOFT FABRIC

- **Microsoft Graph API**: Modify Entra ID user roles and group memberships.

- **Power BI REST API**: Assign workspace roles and configure dataset permissions.

- **Azure Resource Manager API**: Manage security policies and access logs.

5. **Auditing and Monitoring User Access**

    5.1. **Activity Logs and Audit Trails**

    Monitor user activities in Fabric using:

    - **Microsoft Fabric Audit Logs**: Track login attempts, permission changes, and data access.

    - **Power BI Admin Portal**: View detailed usage reports and security incidents.

    - **Azure Monitor**: Set up alerts for suspicious activities.

    5.2. **Identifying and Revoking Unused Access**

    - **Access Reviews**: Regularly review permissions to revoke unnecessary access.

    - **Just-in-Time Access**: Grant temporary permissions instead of permanent roles.

    - **Usage Analytics**: Identify inactive users and optimize role assignments.

6. **Best Practices for User and Access Management**

    1. **Follow the Principle of Least Privilege (PoLP)**: Grant users the minimum access needed.

    2. **Use Entra ID Groups Instead of Individual User Assignments**: Easier to manage.

    3. **Enable Multi-Factor Authentication (MFA)**: Prevent unauthorized access.

    4. **Regularly Review Permissions and Audit Logs**: Identify security risks.

    5. **Enforce Data Loss Prevention (DLP) Policies**: Protect sensitive data.

    6. **Use Row-Level Security (RLS) and Sensitivity Labels**: Control access to data dynamically.

    7. **Implement Conditional Access Policies**: Restrict access based on risk levels.

    8. **Automate Access Management with Power Automate and APIs**: Reduce manual effort.

    9. **Educate Users on Security Best Practices**: Reduce risks from human errors.

    10. **Monitor External User Access Regularly**: Prevent unauthorized data sharing.

Data Security and Compliance in Microsoft Fabric

Ensuring data security and compliance in Microsoft Fabric is essential for protecting sensitive information, maintaining regulatory compliance, and mitigating security risks. This section provides an in-depth guide on implementing security policies, encryption techniques, data governance strategies, and compliance frameworks to safeguard data in Microsoft Fabric.

1. **Data Security Architecture in Microsoft Fabric**

    Microsoft Fabric offers a **multi-layered security model** to protect data at different levels:

    - **Identity and Access Management (IAM):** Uses **Microsoft Entra ID** for authentication, role-based access control (RBAC), and conditional access policies
    - **Data Protection Mechanisms**: Includes encryption at rest and in transit, sensitivity labels, and row-level security (RLS)
    - **Monitoring and Threat Detection**: Uses **Microsoft Defender for Cloud**, **Azure Monitor**, and **audit logs** for tracking security events
    - **Compliance and Governance**: Enforces industry-standard compliance frameworks such as **GDPR, HIPAA, ISO 27001, and SOC 2**

2. **Data Encryption and Protection**

    2.1. **Encryption at Rest and in Transit**

    Encryption ensures that data remains secure even if it is intercepted or accessed by unauthorized users.

- **At Rest Encryption**
    - Microsoft Fabric encrypts all stored data using **Microsoft-managed keys** by default.
    - Organizations can also implement **Customer-Managed Keys (CMK)** using **Azure Key Vault** for greater control.
    - Data stored in **OneLake** is encrypted using **AES-256 encryption**.
- **In Transit Encryption**
    - Fabric enforces **TLS 1.2/1.3 encryption** for all data transmitted between services.
    - **Private Link** ensures that data never leaves Microsoft's secure network.

2.2. **Data Masking and Obfuscation**

- **Dynamic Data Masking (DDM)**: Masks sensitive data dynamically to prevent unauthorized access while allowing certain users to see full data
- **Column-Level Encryption**: Encrypts specific columns (e.g., PII, financial data) while leaving other data accessible
- **Data Tokenization**: Replaces sensitive data with randomly generated values to prevent exposure

3. **Access Control and Data Permissions**

   3.1. **Role-Based Access Control (RBAC)**

   RBAC in Fabric ensures that users have the appropriate level of access based on their role.

Role	Permissions
Admin	Full control over security settings and data permissions.
Data Owner	Can manage datasets, apply security policies, and share data.
Data Steward	Responsible for data governance, compliance, and classification.
Data Consumer	Can only view and analyze reports without modifying data.

   3.2. **Row-Level Security (RLS)**

   - Restricts access to specific rows in a dataset based on user roles.
   - Example: A sales manager sees data for their **region only**, while the CEO sees **all data**.
   - Implemented using **DAX filters in Power BI** or **SQL security policies**.

   3.3. **Column-Level Security (CLS)**

   - Restricts access to specific **columns** within a dataset.
   - Example: **Salary information** is hidden for regular employees but visible to HR personnel.

3.4. **Object-Level Security (OLS)**

- Controls visibility of **entire tables or objects** within a dataset.
- Example: **Finance tables** are only accessible to finance teams.

4. **Data Loss Prevention (DLP) and Sensitivity Labels**

    4.1. **Data Loss Prevention (DLP) Policies**

    DLP policies prevent accidental data leaks and unauthorized data sharing.

    - **Block Sharing of Sensitive Data**
        - Prevent users from **emailing** or **copying sensitive data** outside Fabric.
        - Set alerts for **policy violations** in Microsoft Purview.
    - **Monitor and Restrict Data Movement**
        - Use **DLP policies in Microsoft Defender for Cloud Apps** to prevent unauthorized transfers.
        - Restrict **copying and pasting** of sensitive data between applications.

    4.2. **Sensitivity Labels**

    Sensitivity labels **classify** and **protect** data based on its confidentiality level.

Label	Description
Public	No restrictions, can be shared freely.
Internal	Restricted to employees within the organization.
Confidential	Requires encryption, limited sharing permissions.
Highly Confidential	Strongest encryption, strictest access controls.

- **Automatic Labeling**: AI-powered detection assigns labels based on content analysis.
- **Manual Labeling**: Users manually tag reports, dashboards, or datasets.
- **Policy-Based Labeling**: Enforces labeling based on compliance requirements.

5. **Compliance Frameworks and Regulatory Standards**

    5.1. **Microsoft Fabric Compliance Certifications**

    Microsoft Fabric complies with several **global** and **industry-specific** standards:

Compliance Framework	Description
GDPR (General Data Protection Regulation)	Ensures user privacy and data protection for EU citizens.
HIPAA (Health Insurance Portability and Accountability Act)	Protects patient health information in healthcare organizations.
ISO 27001	International standard for information security management.

(continued)

CHAPTER 5   ADMINISTER AND GOVERN MICROSOFT FABRIC

Compliance Framework	Description
SOC 2	Ensures controls for data security, confidentiality, and privacy.
CCPA (California Consumer Privacy Act)	Similar to GDPR, but applies to California residents.
FedRAMP	US government compliance framework for cloud security.

5.2. **Compliance Monitoring and Reporting**

- **Microsoft Purview Compliance Manager**: Provides real-time compliance scores and remediation actions.

- **Audit Logs and Access Reports**: Tracks all user activities for security auditing.

- **Data Retention Policies**: Enforces automatic data deletion or archiving based on compliance requirements.

6. **Threat Detection and Security Monitoring**

    6.1. **Security Alerts and Incident Response**

    - **Microsoft Defender for Cloud**: Detect threats and anomalies in Fabric workloads.

    - **Azure Sentinel**: Provide SIEM (Security Information and Event Management) capabilities.

    - **Incident Response Playbooks**: Automate responses to detected threats.

6.2. **Insider Threat Detection**

- **Audit User Behavior:** Identify **suspicious access patterns**.
- **Anomaly Detection:** Use AI-based analytics to detect potential insider threats.
- **Just-in-Time Access (JIT):** Reduce the risk of long-term high-privilege access.

6.3. **Logging and Auditing**

- **Microsoft Fabric Audit Logs:** Track **login attempts, data access, and security events**.
- **Azure Monitor and Log Analytics:** Provide centralized logging and dashboards.
- **Automated Alerts:** Notify administrators of **unusual security activities**.

7. **Backup, Disaster Recovery, and Business Continuity**

    7.1. **Backup Strategies**

    - **Automated Backups:** Fabric supports **daily and incremental backups**.
    - **Snapshot Backups:** Save copies of critical datasets for **point-in-time recovery**.
    - **Geo-Redundant Storage (GRS):** Ensures data is backed up across multiple regions.

    7.2. **Disaster Recovery (DR) Planning**

    - **Failover and High Availability:** Automatically redirects traffic during outages.

- **Replication Strategies**: Uses **active-passive or active-active replication** for redundancy.
- **Business Continuity Planning (BCP)**: Defines roles and procedures for data recovery.

7.3. **Data Retention and Archival Policies**

- **Short-Term Retention**: Keeps recent backups for quick recovery.
- **Long-Term Archival**: Moves older datasets to cold storage for regulatory compliance.
- **Legal Hold Policies**: Prevents data deletion for ongoing investigations.

Monitoring and Performance Optimization in Microsoft Fabric

Effective monitoring and performance optimization are crucial for maintaining the efficiency, reliability, and scalability of Microsoft Fabric. This section covers tools, techniques, and best practices for tracking system performance, identifying bottlenecks, optimizing workloads, and ensuring high availability.

1. **Monitoring Microsoft Fabric Components**

    1.1. **Overview of Monitoring in Microsoft Fabric**

    Monitoring in Microsoft Fabric involves tracking the health, performance, and security of various components, including

- **Workspaces**: Managing datasets, reports, and dataflows
- **OneLake Storage:** Monitoring data ingestion and retrieval speed
- **Compute Resources**: Tracking CPU, memory, and resource utilization
- **Data Pipelines:** Ensuring smooth execution of dataflows and transformations
- **Security and Access Logs**: Auditing user activity for compliance

1.2. **Key Monitoring Tools in Microsoft Fabric**

Tool	Purpose
Microsoft Fabric Admin Portal	Provides an overview of service health, capacity usage, and user activity.
Microsoft Purview	Tracks data lineage, sensitivity labels, and compliance violations.
Azure Monitor	Offers real-time telemetry, log analytics, and alerting for Fabric workloads.
Power BI Performance Analyzer	Analyzes report rendering times and query performance.
Microsoft Defender for Cloud	Detects security threats and vulnerabilities.
Fabric Capacity Metrics App	Monitors capacity usage, refresh failures, and dataset performance.

CHAPTER 5   ADMINISTER AND GOVERN MICROSOFT FABRIC

2. **Performance Optimization for Queries and Data Processing**

    2.1. **Optimizing Query Performance**

    Slow queries can lead to performance bottlenecks. The following techniques improve query efficiency:

    2.1.1. **Indexing and Partitioning**

    - **Create Indexes on Large Tables**: Improves query speed by reducing full table scans.
    - **Partition Large Tables**: Splits data into manageable chunks for faster retrieval.
    - **Use Clustered Columnstore Indexes**: Enhances performance for analytical queries.

    2.1.2. **Query Optimization Techniques**

    - **Minimize Data Movement**: Avoid excessive joins and unnecessary calculations in reports.
    - **Reduce Use of SELECT**: Select only required columns.
    - **Optimize DAX Expressions**: Use **SUMX**, **CALCULATE**, and **FILTER** efficiently.
    - **Use DirectQuery When Necessary**: Reduce dataset size and speed up queries.

    2.2. **Performance Tuning for Data Pipelines**

    Efficient data pipelines ensure smooth ETL (Extract, Transform, Load) operations.

2.2.1. Optimize Dataflows and Pipelines

- **Use Incremental Refresh**: Refresh only new or modified data to save processing time.
- **Minimize Data Transformation Steps**: Perform complex transformations at the source instead of in Fabric.
- **Leverage Parallel Processing**: Run multiple transformations simultaneously.
- **Monitor Data Pipeline Logs**: Identify bottlenecks using Azure Monitor.

2.2.2. Data Storage Optimization

- **Use Delta Tables in OneLake**: Improve read/write performance for large datasets.
- **Enable Compression**: Reduce storage costs and enhances retrieval speed.
- **Avoid Storing Unnecessary Data**: Archive or purge old datasets.

3. Resource and Capacity Management

3.1. Managing Fabric Compute Capacity

Microsoft Fabric operates on a capacity-based model, where compute resources are allocated based on demand.

- **Monitor Fabric Capacity Usage**: Use the Fabric Capacity Metrics App to track utilization.

- **Allocate Resources Based on Workload Priorities**: Assign higher capacity to critical workloads.
- **Autoscale Compute Resources**: Enable autoscaling to handle fluctuating demands.
- **Optimize Memory and CPU Utilization**: Adjust workload execution plans for efficiency.

3.2. Scaling Strategies

Scaling ensures that Microsoft Fabric can handle increa ing workloads without performance degradation.

Scaling Method	Description
Vertical Scaling	Increase memory and CPU resources to handle larger workloads.
Horizontal Scaling	Distribute workloads across multiple compute nodes for better efficiency.
Load Balancing	Distribute queries and reports evenly to avoid bottlenecks.
Serverless Scaling	Utilize Fabric's serverless architecture to dynamically allocate resources.

4. Monitoring and Optimizing Data Refresh Performance

4.1. Monitoring Refresh Performance

Data refresh failures can disrupt reporting and analytics. Key techniques for monitoring include

- **Track Refresh History**: View refresh success/failure rates in the Fabric Admin Portal.

- **Analyze Refresh Duration**: Identify slow data sources or transformation steps.

- **Set Refresh Alerts**: Receive notifications for failures or delays.

4.2. **Optimizing Data Refresh**

- **Reduce Data Source Query Complexity**: Optimize SQL queries before refreshing.

- **Use Hybrid Tables**: Combine Import mode (fast queries) and DirectQuery (real-time data).

- **Limit Refresh Frequency**: Avoid unnecessary refreshes that consume resources.

- **Use Power Automate for Scheduled Refreshes**: Automate refreshes at off-peak hours.

5. **Logging and Auditing for Performance Monitoring**

    5.1. **Log Management in Microsoft Fabric**

    Maintaining logs helps diagnose issues and optimize performance.

Log Type	Purpose
Activity Logs	Tracks user actions, such as dataset refreshes and report views.
Error Logs	Captures failures in data pipelines, refresh errors, and query timeouts.
Performance Logs	Records CPU, memory, and query execution metrics.
Security Logs	Monitors unauthorized access and compliance violations.

5.2. **Using Azure Monitor and Log Analytics**

- **Query Log Data**: Use Kusto Query Language (KQL) to analyze log data in Azure Monitor.
- **Set Up Automated Alerts**: Receive notifications for performance anomalies.
- **Generate Performance Dashboards**: Visualize logs using Power BI for proactive monitoring.

6. **Ensuring High Availability and Disaster Recovery**

    6.1. **High Availability Strategies**

    Microsoft Fabric provides built-in redundancy and failover mechanisms to prevent downtime.

    - **Geo-Replication**: Data is automatically replicated across multiple Azure regions.
    - **Automatic Failover**: Redirects workloads to backup servers during outages.
    - **Multi-Region Deployment**: Distributes workloads across different data centers.

6.2. Disaster Recovery Planning

- **Regular Backups**: Schedule automatic backups of critical data.
- **Data Snapshotting**: Save snapshots for quick recovery.
- **Test Disaster Recovery Plans**: Simulate failures to validate recovery procedures.

7. Automating Performance Optimization

7.1. Automating Performance Monitoring

- **Use Power Automate for Automated Workflows**: Trigger alerts based on performance metrics.
- **AI-Powered Anomaly Detection**: Leverage Azure AI to detect unusual patterns.
- **Schedule Performance Reports**: Automate report generation for capacity and usage trends.

7.2. Self-Healing and Auto-Tuning

- **Automated Indexing**: Fabric automatically adjusts indexes for optimized queries.
- **Self-Healing Pipelines**: Detects and fixes data pipeline failures.
- **Auto-Scaling Compute Resources**: Adjusts processing power dynamically.

CHAPTER 5   ADMINISTER AND GOVERN MICROSOFT FABRIC

Governance Best Practices in Microsoft Fabric

Governance is a critical component of Microsoft Fabric, ensuring that data remains secure, compliant, and accessible to the right users while preventing unauthorized access and data misuse. A well-structured governance model enhances data integrity, streamlines administrative processes, and ensures adherence to organizational and regulatory compliance standards such as GDPR, HIPAA, and ISO 27001.

This chapter provides best practices for governance in Microsoft Fabric, focusing on role-based access control (RBAC), data classification, policy enforcement, compliance monitoring, auditability, and continuous governance improvement.

1. **Establishing a Governance Framework**

    1.1. **Understanding the Importance of Data Governance**

    Data governance in Microsoft Fabric refers to the set of policies, roles, responsibilities, and processes that ensure the effective management of data assets within an organization. Effective data governance leads to

    - **Enhanced Data Quality**: Ensures consistency, accuracy, and completeness of data across datasets.
    - **Regulatory Compliance**: Helps organizations adhere to legal and regulatory standards.
    - **Security and Risk Mitigation**: Reduces risks associated with unauthorized access, data breaches, and policy violations.

- **Operational Efficiency**: Ensures seamless collaboration between data analysts, engineers, and administrators while maintaining control over access and modifications.

- **Cost Optimization**: Reduces storage and compute costs by eliminating redundant data and enforcing efficient data management policies.

1.2. **Key Components of a Governance Framework**

A strong governance framework should include the following elements:

Governance Component	Description
Data Ownership	Assigns ownership of data assets to responsible individuals or teams.
Role-Based Access Control (RBAC)	Defines access permissions based on user roles and responsibilities.
Data Classification	Categorizes data based on sensitivity and regulatory requirements.
Audit and Logging Mechanisms	Tracks user activities, modifications, and access history.
Policy Management	Enforces rules related to data usage, retention, and security.
Compliance Monitoring	Ensures adherence to legal and regulatory standards.
Monitoring and Reporting	Uses dashboards and analytics to assess governance effectiveness.

A governance framework should be continuously updated to accommodate new business requirements and regulatory changes.

2. **Role-Based Access Control (RBAC) and Permissions**

    2.1. **Implementing Role-Based Access Control**

    RBAC helps organizations enforce the **principle of least privilege (PoLP)** by granting users only the access they need to perform their tasks.

    2.1.1. **Defining User Roles and Responsibilities**

    Microsoft Fabric supports role-based access control by assigning specific roles to users and managing permissions through Microsoft Entra ID (formerly Azure Active Directory).

Role	Permissions and Responsibilities
Fabric Admin	Full access to manage security, compliance, workspaces, and settings.
Data Owner	Manages dataset permissions, data security, and access policies.
Data Steward	Ensures data quality, governance, and compliance.
Data Analyst	Access to datasets for reporting and analysis but cannot modify permissions.
Viewer	Read-only access to reports and dashboards.

2.1.2. Assigning and Managing Permissions

- **Use Entra ID Groups**: Assign roles at the group level instead of individual users for easier management.

- **Apply Row-Level Security (RLS)**: Restrict access to specific data subsets based on user roles.

- **Enable Multi-Factor Authentication (MFA)**: Strengthen security by requiring additional authentication layers.

2.2. Policy-Based Access Control (PBAC)

Beyond RBAC, organizations can enforce policy-based access controls to dynamically assign permissions based on specific conditions such as **data classification, location, or time-based restrictions**.

3. Data Classification and Sensitivity Labels

3.1. Importance of Data Classification

Data classification helps organizations categorize data based on **sensitivity and compliance requirements**. Microsoft Purview provides **data classification capabilities** to help enforce governance policies.

Classification Level	Description	Examples
Public	Data that can be freely shared outside the organization.	Blog posts, public reports.
Internal	Information meant for internal use only.	Employee handbooks, non-sensitive reports.
Confidential	Sensitive data requiring controlled access.	Customer data, sales records.
Restricted	Highly sensitive data requiring strict protection.	PII, financial records, medical data.

3.2. **Implementing Sensitivity Labels in Microsoft Fabric**

- **Define Sensitivity Labels in Microsoft Purview** to classify datasets automatically.
- **Use Data Loss Prevention (DLP) policies** to prevent sensitive data from being shared externally.
- **Enforce Encryption Policies** for all confidential and restricted data.

4. **Data Lineage and Auditability**

    4.1. **Tracking Data Lineage**

    Data lineage ensures that organizations can **track data origins, transformations, and usage** within Microsoft Fabric.

    Key Features of Data Lineage in Microsoft Fabric:

- **Dataset Dependencies**: Track how datasets, reports, and dashboards interact.
- **Data Source Visibility**: Identify the source of data for auditing and compliance.
- **Automated Data Lineage Tracking**: Microsoft Purview can automatically document data lineage.

4.2. **Audit Logging and Monitoring**

Audit logs are critical for tracking user activities, ensuring security, and maintaining compliance.

Audit Log Type	Purpose
User Access Logs	Track who accessed or modified datasets.
Data Modification Logs	Record changes made to data.
Security Logs	Monitor failed login attempts, unauthorized access.

- **Enable Microsoft Defender for Cloud** to monitor security threats.
- **Use Azure Monitor and Log Analytics** for real-time insights.

5. **Policy Enforcement and Compliance Monitoring**

   5.1. **Defining Governance Policies**

   Organizations should establish governance policies for

- **Data Retention**: Define retention periods for different data types.
- **Data Sharing**: Restrict external sharing of confidential datasets.
- **Data Masking**: Hide sensitive information in reports.
- **Encryption**: Enforce encryption on all sensitive data.

5.2. **Implementing Data Loss Prevention (DLP) in Microsoft Fabric**

- **Configure DLP Policies in Microsoft Purview** to prevent unauthorized data sharing.
- **Use Conditional Access Policies** to block access based on location, device, or risk level.

6. **Monitoring and Continuous Governance Improvement**

    6.1. **Governance Dashboards and Analytics**
    - **Set up Power BI Dashboards** for real-time governance insights.
    - **Monitor Compliance Reports** to assess adherence to regulations.

    6.2. **Automating Governance Processes**
    - **Use Power Automate for Policy Enforcement**: Automate alerts and corrective actions.

- **Leverage AI for Anomaly Detection**: Use machine learning to detect unusual data access patterns.

- **Schedule Periodic Governance Audits**: Regularly assess and improve governance policies.

Chapter Summary

Microsoft Fabric administration ensures **secure, efficient, and compliant** management of data, users, and system resources.

- **User and Access Management** involves role-based access control (RBAC), policy-based access control (PBAC), multi-factor authentication (MFA), and row-level security (RLS) to ensure only authorized users can access data.

- **Data Security and Compliance** focus on encryption, data classification, sensitivity labels, and regulatory compliance with standards such as GDPR, HIPAA, and ISO 27001. Microsoft Purview helps manage security policies and data protection measures.

- **Monitoring and Performance Optimization** involve real-time system performance tracking, workload management, resource optimization, and proactive issue resolution using tools like Azure Monitor and Microsoft Defender for Cloud.

- **Governance Best Practices** include defining a governance framework, implementing policy enforcement, tracking data lineage, conducting regular audits, and using automation to maintain data integrity, security, and compliance.

- A well-structured governance model improves **data quality, security, collaboration, and operational efficiency**, ensuring that Microsoft Fabric runs smoothly while maintaining compliance with organizational and industry standards.

CHAPTER 6

Practice Tests and Exam Strategies

Chapter Overview

Chapter 5 was designed to equip candidates with the necessary tools to excel in the DP-600 certification exam. This chapter provides structured practice tests that align with the exam objectives, allowing candidates to familiarize themselves with key concepts, question formats, and real-world scenarios. Additionally, a dedicated section on exam preparation strategies ensures that candidates develop effective study habits, manage their time efficiently, and leverage the right resources to maximize their chances of success.

The first practice test focuses on Data Warehousing, covering essential aspects such as data storage, lakehouse architecture, query performance optimization, security, and data integration techniques. These questions help candidates gain a deeper understanding of managing data warehouse environments in Microsoft Fabric, ensuring they can handle complex data processing and optimization tasks effectively.

The second practice test emphasizes Semantic Models and Analytics, a fundamental component of Power BI. This section helps candidates develop expertise in constructing efficient data models, optimizing DAX queries, implementing row-level security, and creating insightful visualizations. By working through these questions, candidates will enhance their ability to build high-performing analytical solutions that drive meaningful business insights.

Beyond practice tests, this chapter provides a comprehensive guide to exam preparation strategies and tips. Candidates are encouraged to review official Microsoft documentation, set up hands-on practice environments, and participate in study groups. Effective time management techniques, mock exams, and structured study plans are emphasized to ensure candidates cover all exam objectives thoroughly. On exam day, strategies such as reading questions carefully, eliminating incorrect answers, and managing time effectively will help candidates stay confident and focused.

By integrating these practice tests and preparation strategies, candidates will be well-prepared to tackle the DP-600 exam with confidence. This chapter not only reinforces technical knowledge but also instills the right mindset and approach to certification success.

Question Types Breakdown

The DP-600: Microsoft Fabric Analytics Engineer Associate exam includes a variety of question formats designed to assess both theoretical understanding and practical application. Familiarizing yourself with these question types will help reduce surprises on exam day and enable you to apply effective test-taking strategies. Below is a breakdown of the most common question formats you'll encounter:

1. **Multiple Choice Questions (Single and Multiple Answers)**

    Format

    These questions present a statement or scenario followed by a list of options. Some may have **one correct answer**, while others require you to select **multiple correct answers**.

Tips for Tackling Multiple Choice

- Carefully read the question stem—especially if it says "Choose all that apply."
- Eliminate clearly incorrect options first to narrow your choices.
- Watch for **absolute words** like "always," "never," "only"—these often indicate wrong choices.
- If unsure, mark the question for review and return to it later (if time allows).

Example

Which of the following components are part of Microsoft Fabric's lakehouse architecture? (Choose two)

2. **Drag and Drop**

Format

You'll be asked to **match items** or **arrange steps** in the correct order by dragging options into appropriate targets or sequences.

Tips for Tackling Drag and Drop

- Visualize real-world processes (e.g., data pipeline steps) to determine logical order.
- Try to match terms with the appropriate categories based on definitions or usage.
- Use process-of-elimination by placing known items first, then working out the remaining.

Example

Match the Microsoft Fabric component with its function:

Fabric Component	Function
Lakehouse	?
Warehouse	?
Power BI	?

3. **Case Studies**

   Format

   These consist of a **long scenario**, often with multiple tabs (background, requirements, technical details), followed by **multiple questions** related to the same scenario.

   Tips for Tackling Case Studies

   - Start by scanning the **questions first** to know what to look for in the case material.
   - Pay attention to **requirements and constraints** (e.g., performance, budget, security).
   - Don't bring outside assumptions; rely only on the information provided in the case.
   - Case studies are often time-consuming, so **manage time** efficiently.

Example

A case might describe a company migrating to Microsoft Fabric and needing real-time analytics. Questions will test your ability to choose the right ingestion, transformation, and visualization solutions.

4. **Scenario-Based Questions**

Format

These questions present a **real-world business problem or technical challenge**, often requiring a **best-practice or optimal solution**. Some questions may have **more than one plausible answer**.

Tips for Tackling Scenario-Based Questions

- Identify the **goal**: Are they optimizing performance? Securing data? Reducing costs?

- Select answers aligned with **Microsoft's recommended practices**, even if another choice seems technically correct.

- Choose the solution that's **most scalable, maintainable, and secure**—not just the one that "works."

Example

Your organization needs to implement row-level security for a Power BI dataset built on a Fabric Lakehouse. What is the best approach to enforce dynamic user-based access?

5. **Dropdown Select (Select-in-Place)**

   Format

   In these questions, you'll be given a sentence or code snippet with one or more **blanks**, and each blank has a **dropdown menu**. You must select the most appropriate option from each dropdown.

   Tips for Tackling Dropdown Questions

   - Read the entire sentence or code snippet before selecting an option.
   - Ensure your choices make sense **together**, not just in isolation.
   - Be cautious: once you make a selection and move to the next question, you **cannot return** to change your answer (in most cases).
   - Choose your answers confidently, but review them **before clicking "Next."**

6. **Hotspot (Yes/No or True/False)**

   Format

   Hotspot questions present a **statement or configuration screenshot**, and you're required to answer **Yes or No** (or True/False) for one or multiple items. These too are often **not revisitable** once submitted.

   Tips for Tackling Hotspot Questions

   - Treat these as **binary decisions**, but don't rush—read each carefully.
   - Think in terms of **best practice** or **expected behavior in Microsoft Fabric**.

CHAPTER 6   PRACTICE TESTS AND EXAM STRATEGIES

- Since you cannot revisit, **double-check your reasoning** before submitting.
- If the scenario includes a screenshot, **look for visual cues** (like permissions, toggle settings, DAX expressions, etc.).

Summary Table: Question Types at a Glance

Question Type	Can Revisit?	Strategy Tip
Multiple Choice	✓	Eliminate wrong options, mark for review
Drag and Drop	✓	Use logic and known processes to arrange
Case Study	✓	Scan questions first, note key constraints
Scenario-Based	✓	Think best-practice, scalable, and secure
Dropdown Select	✗	Review thoroughly before submission
Hotspot (Yes/No)	✗	Be cautious; rely on clear product knowledge

Practice Test 1: Data Warehousing

Question 1

You are designing a data warehouse for a retail company using Microsoft Fabric. The company requires real-time data ingestion and high query performance for analytical reporting. Which storage format should you use in your OneLake data warehouse?

- A) JSON
- B) CSV
- C) Parquet
- D) XML

CHAPTER 6 PRACTICE TESTS AND EXAM STRATEGIES

Answer: C) Parquet

Explanation: Parquet is an optimized columnar storage format that provides better query performance and compression, making it ideal for data warehousing in Microsoft Fabric.

Question 2

Which of the following Microsoft Fabric components is best suited for large-scale data transformation and processing before loading into a data warehouse?

- A) Power BI
- B) Dataflows
- C) Data Factory Pipelines
- D) KQL Database

Answer: C) Data Factory Pipelines

Explanation: Data Factory Pipelines provide a scalable ETL solution that allows for data ingestion, transformation, and orchestration before loading into a data warehouse.

Question 3

You need to optimize your Fabric data warehouse for read-heavy workloads while maintaining low storage costs. What should you do?

- A) Store data in JSON format
- B) Use Delta Tables with partitioning
- C) Use row-based storage instead of columnar storage
- D) Disable caching for queries

Answer: B) Use Delta Tables with partitioning

Explanation: Delta Tables with partitioning help optimize read-heavy workloads by enabling efficient querying and storage management.

CHAPTER 6 PRACTICE TESTS AND EXAM STRATEGIES

Question 4

What is the primary benefit of using OneLake in Microsoft Fabric?

    A) It supports only structured data.

    B) It eliminates the need for ETL processes.

    C) It provides a unified data storage layer for analytics.

    D) It replaces Power BI entirely.

Answer: C) It provides a unified data storage layer for analytics.
Explanation: OneLake serves as a centralized data storage solution, supporting multiple analytics workloads seamlessly.

Question 5

Which indexing strategy improves query performance in a Fabric data warehouse?

    A) Full Table Scan

    B) Clustered Columnstore Index

    C) Hash Index

    D) Primary Key Index

Answer: B) Clustered Columnstore Index
Explanation: A Clustered Columnstore Index significantly improves analytical query performance by compressing data and reducing I/O.

Question 6

Which tool in Microsoft Fabric allows scheduling of data warehouse refreshes?

    A) Power Automate

    B) Data Factory Pipelines

    C) Kusto Query Language (KQL)

    D) OneLake Manager

CHAPTER 6   PRACTICE TESTS AND EXAM STRATEGIES

Answer: B) Data Factory Pipelines
Explanation: Data Factory Pipelines enable automated and scheduled data refreshes in Fabric.

Question 7
Which feature in Fabric enables real-time data ingestion for analytical processing?

    A)   Delta Live Tables

    B)   Streaming Dataflows

    C)   Spark Batch Processing

    D)   Power BI Paginated Reports

Answer: B) Streaming Dataflows
Explanation: Streaming Dataflows provide real-time data ingestion, enabling faster insights from live data sources.

Question 8
Which security feature ensures role-based access control in a Fabric data warehouse?

    A)   Row-Level Security (RLS)

    B)   Shared Access Signatures (SAS)

    C)   Transparent Data Encryption (TDE)

    D)   Azure Firewall

Answer: A) Row-Level Security (RLS)
Explanation: RLS restricts data access at the row level, ensuring different users see only relevant data.

Question 9
Which feature in Fabric helps manage changes in slowly changing dimensions (SCDs)?

    A) Delta Lake Time Travel

    B) Table Partitioning

    C) Azure Synapse Link

    D) Dataflow Snapshots

Answer: A) Delta Lake Time Travel

Explanation: Delta Lake Time Travel allows querying previous versions of a table, making it useful for managing historical changes.

Question 10
What is the best practice for handling schema changes in a Fabric data warehouse?

    A) Use JSON to store schema metadata

    B) Drop and recreate tables frequently

    C) Use Schema Evolution in Delta Tables

    D) Avoid making schema changes

Answer: C) Use Schema Evolution in Delta Tables

Explanation: Schema Evolution in Delta Tables allows automatic adaptation to schema changes, reducing manual intervention.

Practice Test 2: Semantic Models and Analytics

Question 1
In Microsoft Fabric, you need to create a highly optimized semantic model for Power BI reporting. What is the recommended storage mode?

A) Import Mode

B) DirectQuery Mode

C) Composite Mode

D) On-Premises Mode

Answer: A) Import Mode

Explanation: Import Mode provides the best performance for Power BI reports by caching data in-memory for fast query execution.

Question 2

Which of the following DAX functions can be used to create a measure that calculates the year-over-year sales growth?

A) SUMX

B) CALCULATE

C) SAMEPERIODLASTYEAR

D) CONCATENATE

Answer: C) SAMEPERIODLASTYEAR

Explanation: SAMEPERIODLASTYEAR helps compare the same period in the previous year, making it useful for calculating year-over-year growth.

Question 3

What is the primary benefit of using aggregations in Power BI semantic models?

A) Reduces report page load times

B) Increases data refresh speed

C) Reduces the need for relationships in models

D) Enables real-time streaming of data

Answer: A) Reduces report page load times
Explanation: Aggregations precompute summaries, allowing Power BI to query smaller datasets and significantly improve performance.

Question 4
Which type of Power BI relationship allows filtering in both directions between two tables?

- A) One-to-Many (Single)
- B) One-to-Many (Both)
- C) Many-to-One
- D) One-to-One

Answer: B) One-to-Many (Both)
Explanation: A bi-directional relationship allows filtering from both related tables, improving flexibility in reporting.

Question 5
What is the recommended way to improve performance in a DirectQuery Power BI model?

- A) Enable bidirectional cross-filtering for all relationships
- B) Reduce the number of columns in tables
- C) Use DAX calculated columns instead of pre-calculated columns in the data source
- D) Avoid indexing tables in the database

Answer: B) Reduce the number of columns in tables
Explanation: Reducing the number of columns minimizes the data load, leading to improved performance in DirectQuery mode.

CHAPTER 6   PRACTICE TESTS AND EXAM STRATEGIES

Question 6
Which of the following storage modes in Power BI allows for a combination of Import and DirectQuery data sources?

    A) Import Mode

    B) Composite Mode

    C) Live Connection Mode

    D) DirectQuery Mode

Answer: B) Composite Mode
Explanation: Composite Mode enables the use of both Import and DirectQuery, offering flexibility and performance optimization.

Question 7
Which Power BI feature allows you to restrict data access at a row level based on user roles?

    A) Dynamic Data Masking

    B) Row-Level Security (RLS)

    C) Column Encryption

    D) Azure Firewall

Answer: B) Row-Level Security (RLS)
Explanation: RLS filters data based on user roles, ensuring that each user sees only the relevant data.

Question 8
Which DAX function is best suited for calculating a running total in Power BI?

    A) FILTER

    B) RANKX

    C) SUMX

    D) TOTALYTD

Answer: D) TOTALYTD

Explanation: TOTALYTD calculates the year-to-date total of a measure, making it suitable for running totals.

Question 9

Which visualization type is best suited for comparing trends over time in Power BI?

- A) Pie Chart
- B) Bar Chart
- C) Line Chart
- D) Scatter Plot

Answer: C) Line Chart

Explanation: A Line Chart is ideal for visualizing trends over time due to its ability to depict continuous data changes.

Question 10

What is the purpose of the Power BI Performance Analyzer tool?

- A) To create calculated tables
- B) To optimize data models
- C) To measure and analyze report performance
- D) To publish reports to Power BI Service

Answer: C) To measure and analyze report performance

Explanation: Performance Analyzer helps identify bottlenecks and optimize reports for better efficiency.

CHAPTER 6   PRACTICE TESTS AND EXAM STRATEGIES

Try This Question Set

1. What Azure service would you use to orchestrate a data workflow that integrates data from various sources into a central repository?

   A) Azure Data Factory

   B) Azure Synapse Analytics

   C) Azure Logic Apps

   D) Azure Event Grid

2. Which Azure service provides real-time data processing for IoT scenarios?

   A) Azure Stream Analytics

   B) Azure Databricks

   C) Azure Data Lake Storage

   D) Azure Functions

3. Which Azure service can be used to perform advanced analytics on big data?

   A) Azure SQL Database

   B) Azure Databricks

   C) Azure Blob Storage

   D) Azure Event Hub

4. Which Azure service provides built-in metadata management and data governance?

   A) Azure Purview

   B) Azure Data Factory

CHAPTER 6   PRACTICE TESTS AND EXAM STRATEGIES

C) Azure SQL Database

D) Azure Machine Learning

5. To store and process large datasets, which Azure service is most efficient for a data warehouse solution?

   A) Azure Synapse Analytics

   B) Azure Blob Storage

   C) Azure Cosmos DB

   D) Azure Data Lake Storage

6. Which Azure service allows you to analyze data from different sources with built-in machine-learning capabilities?

   A) Azure Cognitive Services

   B) Azure Machine Learning

   C) Azure Stream Analytics

   D) Azure Functions

7. For moving data between on-premises systems and Azure storage, which Azure service is most efficient?

   A) Azure Migrate

   B) Azure Data Factory

   C) Azure Blob Storage

   D) Azure SQL Database

CHAPTER 6   PRACTICE TESTS AND EXAM STRATEGIES

8. Which Azure service provides scalable storage for data analytics workloads?

    A) Azure SQL Database

    B) Azure Data Lake Storage

    C) Azure Event Hub

    D) Azure Functions

9. For real-time data streaming analytics, which Azure service would you recommend?

    A) Azure Stream Analytics

    B) Azure Data Factory

    C) Azure Databricks

    D) Azure Synapse Analytics

10. Which Azure service allows you to manage data pipelines and perform complex data transformations?

    A) Azure Data Factory

    B) Azure Logic Apps

    C) Azure Event Hub

    D) Azure Functions

11. Which Azure service is best suited for managing data governance and metadata in Azure?

    A) Azure Purview

    B) Azure Data Factory

    C) Azure SQL Database

    D) Azure Machine Learning

CHAPTER 6   PRACTICE TESTS AND EXAM STRATEGIES

12. Which Azure service supports big data analytics and real-time streaming for IoT scenarios?

    A) Azure Stream Analytics

    B) Azure Databricks

    C) Azure Data Lake Storage

    D) Azure Functions

13. Which Azure service is optimized for handling semi-structured and unstructured data?

    A) Azure Synapse Analytics

    B) Azure Cognitive Services

    C) Azure Data Lake Storage

    D) Azure Event Hub

14. For a solution involving batch data processing and machine learning, which Azure service is ideal?

    A) Azure Databricks

    B) Azure Synapse Analytics

    C) Azure Machine Learning

    D) Azure Data Factory

15. Which Azure service provides a platform for serverless big data analytics?

    A) Azure Synapse Analytics

    B) Azure Functions

    C) Azure Blob Storage

    D) Azure Stream Analytics

CHAPTER 6   PRACTICE TESTS AND EXAM STRATEGIES

16. Which Azure service is best for managing real-time data processing and event-driven architecture?

    A) Azure Stream Analytics

    B) Azure Functions

    C) Azure Event Grid

    D) Azure Data Factory

17. For managing data across multiple regions, which Azure service should be used?

    A) Azure Synapse Analytics

    B) Azure Data Factory

    C) Azure Data Lake Storage

    D) Azure Blob Storage

18. Which service provides advanced analytics capabilities for complex data processing?

    A) Azure Databricks

    B) Azure Machine Learning

    C) Azure Stream Analytics

    D) Azure Functions

19. Which service is optimized for real-time analytics and event-driven processing?

    A) Azure Event Hub

    B) Azure Stream Analytics

    C) Azure Data Lake Storage

    D) Azure Functions

CHAPTER 6   PRACTICE TESTS AND EXAM STRATEGIES

20. Which Azure service allows for high-performance querying of big datasets?

    A)   Azure SQL Database

    B)   Azure Synapse Analytics

    C)   Azure Data Lake Storage

    D)   Azure Blob Storage

21. For securely sharing data between different departments and organizations, which service would you use?

    A)   Azure Purview

    B)   Azure Data Share

    C)   Azure Stream Analytics

    D)   Azure Functions

22. Which Azure service is designed for managing and orchestrating complex data pipelines?

    A)   Azure Data Factory

    B)   Azure Logic Apps

    C)   Azure Functions

    D)   Azure Databricks

23. Which Azure service is ideal for managing data governance, security, and lineage?

    A)   Azure Purview

    B)   Azure Data Factory

    C)   Azure SQL Database

    D)   Azure Machine Learning

CHAPTER 6   PRACTICE TESTS AND EXAM STRATEGIES

24. For processing and analyzing streaming data at scale, which service is most appropriate?

    A) Azure Stream Analytics

    B) Azure Functions

    C) Azure Databricks

    D) Azure Event Hub

25. Which Azure service allows for real-time data transformation and analytics for IoT devices?

    A) Azure Stream Analytics

    B) Azure Machine Learning

    C) Azure Databricks

    D) Azure Functions

26. Which Azure service is used for real-time data visualization and interactive analytics?

    A) Azure Power BI

    B) Azure Cognitive Services

    C) Azure Data Factory

    D) Azure Event Grid

27. Which service helps in managing complex workflows across multiple data systems?

    A) Azure Logic Apps

    B) Azure Data Factory

    C) Azure Stream Analytics

    D) Azure Functions

CHAPTER 6   PRACTICE TESTS AND EXAM STRATEGIES

28. For managing a hybrid cloud solution involving both on-premises and cloud data, which Azure service is ideal?

    A) Azure Data Factory

    B) Azure Functions

    C) Azure Machine Learning

    D) Azure Databricks

29. Which service allows you to automate machine learning workflows and model deployment?

    A) Azure Machine Learning

    B) Azure Databricks

    C) Azure Cognitive Services

    D) Azure Purview

30. Which Azure service allows for managing metadata and data cataloging across multiple data services?

    A) Azure Purview

    B) Azure Data Factory

    C) Azure Stream Analytics

    D) Azure Functions

31. Which Azure service is designed for high-performance, distributed big data analytics?

    A) Azure Synapse Analytics

    B) Azure Databricks

    C) Azure Data Lake Storage

    D) Azure Functions

CHAPTER 6   PRACTICE TESTS AND EXAM STRATEGIES

32. Which service supports real-time data ingestion from millions of IoT devices?

    A) Azure Event Hub

    B) Azure Stream Analytics

    C) Azure Data Factory

    D) Azure Functions

33. Which Azure service is best for creating data-driven workflows involving automated event-driven processes?

    A) Azure Stream Analytics

    B) Azure Functions

    C) Azure Logic Apps

    D) Azure Machine Learning

34. Which Azure service is used for serverless machine learning operations?

    A) Azure Machine Learning

    B) Azure Functions

    C) Azure Cognitive Services

    D) Azure Databricks

35. Which Azure service provides a unified environment for integrating analytics and big data solutions?

    A) Azure Synapse Analytics

    B) Azure Blob Storage

    C) Azure Stream Analytics

    D) Azure Functions

CHAPTER 6   PRACTICE TESTS AND EXAM STRATEGIES

36. Which Azure service helps with managing and automating complex data workflows at scale?

    A) Azure Logic Apps

    B) Azure Stream Analytics

    C) Azure Data Factory

    D) Azure Functions

37. Which Azure service provides serverless data processing and analytics for large datasets?

    A) Azure Synapse Analytics

    B) Azure Functions

    C) Azure Data Lake Storage

    D) Azure Machine Learning

38. Which Azure service is designed for event-driven data solutions with real-time analytics capabilities?

    A) Azure Event Grid

    B) Azure Stream Analytics

    C) Azure Functions

    D) Azure Data Factory

39. Which Azure service enables high-performance querying across structured and semi-structured data?

    A) Azure Synapse Analytics

    B) Azure Cognitive Services

    C) Azure SQL Database

    D) Azure Data Lake Storage

CHAPTER 6   PRACTICE TESTS AND EXAM STRATEGIES

40. For securely managing data across different environments, which Azure service provides the best solution?

    A) Azure Purview

    B) Azure Stream Analytics

    C) Azure Logic Apps

    D) Azure Machine Learning

41. Which service supports the deployment of real-time machine-learning models?

    A) Azure Databricks

    B) Azure Machine Learning

    C) Azure Functions

    D) Azure Stream Analytics

42. Which Azure service is ideal for managing large-scale data governance and compliance across multiple platforms?

    A) Azure Purview

    B) Azure Synapse Analytics

    C) Azure Data Lake Storage

    D) Azure Functions

43. Which service enables real-time processing of high-volume data streams?

    A) Azure Stream Analytics

    B) Azure Functions

    C) Azure Event Hub

    D) Azure Databricks

CHAPTER 6 PRACTICE TESTS AND EXAM STRATEGIES

44. Which Azure service is optimized for managing data pipelines and integrating data workflows?

    A) Azure Data Factory

    B) Azure Logic Apps

    C) Azure Stream Analytics

    D) Azure Functions

45. For building event-driven architectures involving complex data transformations, which service is best?

    A) Azure Event Grid

    B) Azure Stream Analytics

    C) Azure Functions

    D) Azure Databricks

46. Which Azure service allows you to analyze and monitor data pipelines for optimizing performance?

    A) Azure Monitor

    B) Azure Logic Apps

    C) Azure Stream Analytics

    D) Azure Data Factory

47. Which Azure service provides a scalable platform for managing machine learning models?

    A) Azure Machine Learning

    B) Azure Cognitive Services

    C) Azure Databricks

    D) Azure Functions

CHAPTER 6   PRACTICE TESTS AND EXAM STRATEGIES

48. Which Azure service is used for managing serverless data workflows with event-driven capabilities?

    A) Azure Logic Apps

    B) Azure Stream Analytics

    C) Azure Functions

    D) Azure Data Factory

49. For handling petabyte-scale data analytics, which Azure service would you use?

    A) Azure Synapse Analytics

    B) Azure Data Lake Storage

    C) Azure Blob Storage

    D) Azure Event Hub

50. Which Azure service supports real-time data processing and integration with Azure IoT devices?

    A) Azure Stream Analytics

    B) Azure Functions

    C) Azure Event Grid

    D) Azure Data Factory

Case Study–Based Questions

51. **Case Study**: Contoso Corporation is transitioning its analytics workload to Microsoft Fabric, integrating data from various sources like on-premises databases and SaaS applications. What approach would best ensure seamless data ingestion?

CHAPTER 6   PRACTICE TESTS AND EXAM STRATEGIES

   A) Use Azure Data Factory for ETL processes

   B) Directly upload files to Azure Blob Storage

   C) Leverage Azure Stream Analytics for real-time processing

   D) Utilize Power BI for semantic model creation

52. **Case Study**: Fabrikam Inc. wants to implement a data warehouse using Microsoft Fabric. They require high-performance queries across petabyte-scale datasets. Which service should they prioritize?

   A) Azure Synapse Analytics

   B) Azure Data Explorer

   C) Azure Data Lake Storage

   D) Azure SQL Database

53. **Case Study**: Adventure Works has a variety of data sources and needs a unified semantic model within Microsoft Fabric to provide intuitive insights for non-technical users. What tool should they use?

   A) Power BI

   B) Azure Data Explorer

   C) Azure Synapse Studio

   D) Azure Functions

54. **Case Study**: Litware Inc. wants to create a governance model in Microsoft Fabric to track data lineage and ensure data quality. Which feature would best support this requirement?

CHAPTER 6   PRACTICE TESTS AND EXAM STRATEGIES

   A) Azure Purview

   B) Azure Data Factory

   C) Azure Data Catalog

   D) Azure Stream Analytics

55. **Case Study**: Contoso Corporation requires a scalable solution within Microsoft Fabric to support real-time IoT analytics. What service would best address this?

   A) Azure Event Hubs

   B) Azure Stream Analytics

   C) Azure IoT Central

   D) Azure Functions

56. **Case Study**: Fabrikam is implementing a data warehouse solution using Microsoft Fabric and needs to optimize performance with real-time data analytics. Which approach should they take?

   A) Use Azure Synapse Studio

   B) Enable near real-time streaming with Azure Data Factory

   C) Integrate Azure Machine Learning for predictive analytics

   D) Leverage Azure Event Hubs for data ingestion

57. **Case Study**: Adventure Works needs to manage user permissions and data security across multiple workspaces in Microsoft Fabric. Which feature would provide the most robust governance?

216

CHAPTER 6 PRACTICE TESTS AND EXAM STRATEGIES

A) Azure AD Role-Based Access Control (RBAC)

B) Microsoft Fabric Power BI integration

C) Azure Data Catalog

D) Azure Stream Analytics

58. **Case Study**: Litware Inc. is integrating Azure Cognitive Services with Microsoft Fabric for natural language processing. Which service would be the best fit?

    A) Azure Data Lake

    B) Azure Functions

    C) Azure Machine Learning

    D) Azure Cognitive Search

59. **Case Study**: Contoso Corporation wants to implement a disaster recovery solution for its Microsoft Fabric environment. Which approach is most effective?

    A) Use Azure Site Recovery for data replication

    B) Deploy additional nodes for high availability

    C) Use Azure Backup for snapshots

    D) Implement geo-replication using Azure Data Factory

60. **Case Study**: Fabrikam is dealing with large datasets and needs to optimize data refresh cycles for Power BI reports within Microsoft Fabric. What strategy should they employ?

A) Use Azure Data Factory pipelines with incremental load

B) Enable real-time analytics with Azure Stream Analytics

C) Leverage Azure Synapse Studio for batch processing

D) Utilize Azure Data Lake Storage for data storage

61. **Case Study**: Adventure Works requires real-time analytics for financial dashboards in Microsoft Fabric. Which service is best suited for this?

    A) Azure Functions

    B) Azure Stream Analytics

    C) Azure Data Factory

    D) Azure Blob Storage

62. **Case Study**: Litware Inc. wants to implement a self-service BI solution using Microsoft Fabric. How should they manage user permissions and data access?

    A) Use Azure AD RBAC

    B) Implement Azure Data Share

    C) Utilize Power BI service permissions

    D) Enable Microsoft Fabric workspace access

63. **Case Study**: Contoso Corporation is working on a data mesh architecture within Microsoft Fabric to ensure data interoperability across multiple domains. What tools would help in achieving this?

CHAPTER 6 PRACTICE TESTS AND EXAM STRATEGIES

A) Azure Data Factory

B) Azure Synapse Studio

C) Azure Data Lake Storage

D) Azure Event Hubs

64. **Case Study**: Fabrikam Inc. needs to monitor and optimize performance for their Microsoft Fabric data warehouse. Which tool would provide detailed analytics and insights?

A) Azure Monitor

B) Azure Data Catalog

C) Azure Synapse Studio

D) Azure Stream Analytics

65. **Case Study**: Adventure Works has several data sources and needs a unified governance framework within Microsoft Fabric. What service should they prioritize?

A) Azure Purview

B) Azure Functions

C) Azure AD Role-Based Access Control (RBAC)

D) Azure Data Factory

66. **Case Study**: Litware Inc. is handling large-scale IoT data analytics in Microsoft Fabric. Which service should be prioritized for efficient data ingestion?

A) Azure Event Hubs

B) Azure Functions

C) Azure Data Lake Storage

D) Azure Data Explorer

67. **Case Study**: Contoso Corporation requires real-time insights into customer behavior within Microsoft Fabric. Which service should they use for seamless integration?

    A) Azure Stream Analytics

    B) Azure Functions

    C) Azure Data Factory

    D) Azure Event Grid

68. **Case Study**: Fabrikam needs to ensure that its Microsoft Fabric data warehouse maintains high availability for mission-critical operations. What solution should they implement?

    A) Enable Active Geo-Replication

    B) Use Azure Data Share

    C) Deploy additional nodes

    D) Utilize Azure Backup

69. **Case Study**: Adventure Works is migrating its existing data warehouse to Microsoft Fabric while maintaining existing workflows. What challenges should they prepare for?

    A) Data redundancy

    B) Data inconsistency

    C) High latency

    D) Data governance

CHAPTER 6   PRACTICE TESTS AND EXAM STRATEGIES

70. **Case Study**: Litware Inc. is integrating machine learning models into Microsoft Fabric for predictive analytics. Which tools should they leverage?

    A) Azure Machine Learning

    B) Azure Stream Analytics

    C) Azure Functions

    D) Azure Cognitive Services

71. **Case Study**: Contoso Corporation needs to manage data transformation and ETL processes within Microsoft Fabric for their analytics workloads. Which tool would provide the best solution?

    A) Azure Data Factory

    B) Azure Data Lake

    C) Azure Functions

    D) Power BI

72. **Case Study**: Fabrikam Inc. is optimizing data refresh cycles for its Power BI reports using Microsoft Fabric. Which strategy should they use?

    A) Incremental data refresh using Azure Data Factory

    B) Real-time data streaming via Azure Stream Analytics

    C) Batch processing with Azure Synapse Studio

    D) Direct query mode with Power BI

73. **Case Study**: Adventure Works is handling sensitive customer data within Microsoft Fabric and wants to implement robust data security. Which feature should be used?

    A) Azure AD RBAC

    B) Azure Purview

    C) Azure Data Share

    D) Azure Functions

74. **Case Study**: Litware Inc. requires monitoring and troubleshooting data flow errors within Microsoft Fabric. What tool would be most beneficial?

    A) Azure Monitor

    B) Azure Data Factory

    C) Azure Stream Analytics

    D) Azure Functions

75. **Case Study**: Contoso Corporation is integrating IoT data with Microsoft Fabric for real-time analytics. What architecture considerations should they focus on?

    A) High-performance computing

    B) Scalability and reliability

    C) Data transformation

    D) Data cataloging

76. **Case Study**: Fabrikam is implementing a disaster recovery plan for its Microsoft Fabric environment. What steps should they prioritize?

CHAPTER 6 PRACTICE TESTS AND EXAM STRATEGIES

   A) Data replication

   B) Azure Backup

   C) Geo-replication

   D) Data archiving

77. **Case Study**: Adventure Works needs to create real-time dashboards using Microsoft Fabric. What architectural choices would optimize performance?

   A) Use Azure Stream Analytics

   B) Enable real-time analytics

   C) Leverage Azure Functions

   D) Implement Azure Data Factory pipelines

78. **Case Study**: Litware Inc. is integrating large-scale IoT data into Microsoft Fabric. What tool should be prioritized for efficient data processing?

   A) Azure Data Explorer

   B) Azure Event Hubs

   C) Azure Machine Learning

   D) Azure Functions

79. **Case Study**: Contoso Corporation is using Microsoft Fabric for a centralized data hub. What strategies should be employed for managing governance and security?

   A) Azure AD RBAC

   B) Azure Purview

   C) Azure Data Factory

   D) Azure Stream Analytics

CHAPTER 6   PRACTICE TESTS AND EXAM STRATEGIES

80. **Case Study**: Fabrikam Inc. is expanding its use of Microsoft Fabric for financial analytics and is implementing real-time updates. What steps should be taken to optimize data ingestion?

    A) Leverage Azure Data Factory

    B) Use Azure Stream Analytics

    C) Integrate Azure Event Hubs

    D) Use Power BI Direct Query

81. **Case Study**: Adventure Works is consolidating multiple data sources into Microsoft Fabric. What challenges could arise during data transformation, and how can they be mitigated?

    A) High data redundancy

    B) Data inconsistency

    C) Increased latency

    D) Poor data governance

82. **Case Study**: Litware Inc. needs to manage a self-service BI solution within Microsoft Fabric. How should user permissions and data access be handled?

    A) Azure AD RBAC

    B) Microsoft Fabric workspace access

    C) Azure Data Share

    D) Power BI service permissions

CHAPTER 6   PRACTICE TESTS AND EXAM STRATEGIES

83. **Case Study**: Contoso Corporation requires a data governance framework to ensure data quality and consistency within Microsoft Fabric. What steps should they take?

    A) Implement Azure Purview

    B) Utilize Azure Functions

    C) Use Azure Stream Analytics

    D) Leverage Azure Data Factory

84. **Case Study**: Fabrikam is implementing machine learning models into Microsoft Fabric for predictive analytics. How should they manage the model life cycle?

    A) Monitor model performance using Azure Monitor

    B) Use Azure Data Catalog for metadata management

    C) Implement Azure Machine Learning for model governance

    D) Leverage Power BI for visualizing insights

85. **Case Study**: Adventure Works has several data sources and needs a unified data model within Microsoft Fabric for customer analytics. What considerations should they make for data governance?

    A) Ensure data lineage visibility

    B) Enable incremental data refresh

    C) Integrate real-time analytics

    D) Use Azure Functions for data transformation

CHAPTER 6   PRACTICE TESTS AND EXAM STRATEGIES

86. **Case Study**: Litware Inc. wants to handle IoT data analytics at scale within Microsoft Fabric. Which service should be prioritized?

    A) Azure Data Lake

    B) Azure Event Hubs

    C) Azure Machine Learning

    D) Azure Cognitive Services

87. **Case Study**: Contoso Corporation is scaling its Microsoft Fabric deployment and needs to ensure smooth administration across multiple teams. What best practices should be adopted?

    A) Implement Azure Purview

    B) Use Azure Data Factory for workflows

    C) Enable Azure AD RBAC

    D) Leverage Azure Stream Analytics

88. **Case Study**: Fabrikam is optimizing data refresh cycles for Power BI reports in Microsoft Fabric. What strategy should they adopt?

    A) Use Azure Synapse Studio for batch processing

    B) Enable incremental load using Azure Data Factory

    C) Implement real-time analytics with Azure Stream Analytics

    D) Use Power BI Direct Query mode

CHAPTER 6   PRACTICE TESTS AND EXAM STRATEGIES

89. **Case Study**: Adventure Works is integrating Azure Cognitive Services into Microsoft Fabric for advanced analytics. Which services should they focus on?

    A) Azure Machine Learning

    B) Azure Data Lake

    C) Azure Functions

    D) Azure Cognitive Search

90. **Case Study**: Litware Inc. is handling sensitive customer data in Microsoft Fabric. How should they approach data privacy and compliance?

    A) Implement Azure AD RBAC

    B) Enable Azure Purview

    C) Use Azure Data Catalog

    D) Leverage Power BI for self-service analytics

91. **Case Study**: Contoso Corporation is integrating IoT data with Microsoft Fabric for real-time analytics. What architectural considerations should be made?

    A) High-performance computing

    B) Scalability and reliability

    C) Data transformation

    D) Data cataloging

CHAPTER 6   PRACTICE TESTS AND EXAM STRATEGIES

92. **Case Study**: Fabrikam is implementing a disaster recovery solution for its Microsoft Fabric environment. Which best practices should be followed?

    A)   Data replication

    B)   Azure Backup

    C)   Geo-replication

    D)   Data archiving

93. **Case Study**: Adventure Works is expanding its use of Microsoft Fabric for financial analytics and implementing real-time updates. What steps should be taken to optimize data ingestion?

    A)   Leverage Azure Data Factory

    B)   Use Azure Stream Analytics

    C)   Integrate Azure Event Hubs

    D)   Use Power BI Direct Query

94. **Case Study**: Litware Inc. is managing a self-service BI solution within Microsoft Fabric. How should user permissions and data access be handled?

    A)   Azure AD RBAC

    B)   Microsoft Fabric workspace access

    C)   Azure Data Share

    D)   Power BI service permissions

CHAPTER 6   PRACTICE TESTS AND EXAM STRATEGIES

95. **Case Study**: Contoso Corporation requires a data governance framework to ensure data quality and consistency within Microsoft Fabric. What steps should they take?

    A) Implement Azure Purview

    B) Utilize Azure Functions

    C) Use Azure Stream Analytics

    D) Leverage Azure Data Factory

96. **Case Study**: Fabrikam is integrating machine learning models into Microsoft Fabric for predictive analytics. How should they manage the model life cycle?

    A) Monitor model performance using Azure Monitor

    B) Use Azure Data Catalog for metadata management

    C) Implement Azure Machine Learning for model governance

    D) Leverage Power BI for visualizing insights

97. **Case Study**: Adventure Works has several data sources and needs a unified data model within Microsoft Fabric for customer analytics. What considerations should they make for data governance?

    A) Ensure data lineage visibility

    B) Enable incremental data refresh

    C) Integrate real-time analytics

    D) Use Azure Functions for data transformation

CHAPTER 6   PRACTICE TESTS AND EXAM STRATEGIES

98. **Case Study**: Litware Inc. wants to handle IoT data analytics at scale within Microsoft Fabric. Which service should be prioritized?

    A) Azure Data Lake

    B) Azure Event Hubs

    C) Azure Machine Learning

    D) Azure Cognitive Services

99. **Case Study**: Contoso Corporation is scaling its Microsoft Fabric deployment and needs to ensure smooth administration across multiple teams. What best practices should be adopted?

    A) Implement Azure Purview

    B) Use Azure Data Factory for workflows

    C) Enable Azure AD RBAC

    D) Leverage Azure Stream Analytics

100. **Case Study**: Fabrikam is optimizing data refresh cycles for Power BI reports in Microsoft Fabric. What strategy should they adopt?

    A) Use Azure Synapse Studio for batch processing

    B) Enable incremental load using Azure Data Factory

    C) Implement real-time analytics with Azure Stream Analytics

    D) Use Power BI Direct Query mode

CHAPTER 6   PRACTICE TESTS AND EXAM STRATEGIES

Answers for 1–50 Questions

1. **A**
2. **A**
3. **B**
4. **A**
5. **A**
6. **B**
7. **B**
8. **B**
9. **A**
10. **A**
11. **A**
12. **A**
13. **C**
14. **A**
15. **A**
16. **B**
17. **C**
18. **A**
19. **A**
20. **B**
21. **B**
22. **A**

23. **A**
24. **A**
25. **A**
26. **A**
27. **A**
28. **A**
29. **A**
30. **A**
31. **B**
32. **A**
33. **C**
34. **A**
35. **A**
36. **C**
37. **B**
38. **A**
39. **A**
40. **A**
41. **B**
42. **A**
43. **A**
44. **A**
45. **D**

CHAPTER 6 PRACTICE TESTS AND EXAM STRATEGIES

46. **D**
47. **A**
48. **C**
49. **A**
50. **A**

Answers for 51–100 Case Study–Based Questions

51. **A**
52. **C**
53. **A**
54. **A**
55. **B**
56. **A**
57. **A**
58. **D**
59. **C**
60. **A**
61. **B**
62. **A**
63. **A**
64. **A**
65. **B**
66. **A**
67. **A**

CHAPTER 6   PRACTICE TESTS AND EXAM STRATEGIES

68. **C**
69. **D**
70. **A**
71. **A**
72. **A**
73. **A**
74. **A**
75. **B**
76. **C**
77. **B**
78. **A**
79. **A**
80. **A**
81. **B**
82. **A**
83. **A**
84. **C**
85. **A**
86. **B**
87. **C**
88. **B**
89. **A**
90. **B**

CHAPTER 6   PRACTICE TESTS AND EXAM STRATEGIES

91. **B**
92. **C**
93. **B**
94. **A**
95. **A**
96. **C**
97. **A**
98. **B**
99. **C**
100. **B**

Exam Preparation Strategies and Tips

1. **Understand Exam Objectives**
    - Carefully review the DP-600 exam skills outline provided by Microsoft.
    - Focus on key topics such as data warehousing, semantic models, DAX, Power BI, and Microsoft Fabric.
    - Ensure you understand the exam format, including the types of questions (multiple-choice, case studies, drag-and-drop, etc.).

CHAPTER 6   PRACTICE TESTS AND EXAM STRATEGIES

2. **Hands-on Practice**

    - Set up a Microsoft Fabric environment and explore its components, such as OneLake, Data Factory, and Power BI.

    - Work with different storage formats and transformation techniques.

    - Practice writing and optimizing DAX formulas for various business scenarios.

    - Build and optimize semantic models in Power BI to get comfortable with relationships, aggregations, and performance tuning.

3. **Time Management**

    - Create a structured study plan with allocated time for each exam topic.

    - Spend extra time on topics where you feel less confident.

    - Use the elimination method in the exam to quickly discard incorrect answers and improve response time.

    - Practice time-bound mock tests to simulate the actual exam environment.

4. **Use Official and Reliable Resources**

    - Leverage Microsoft Learn modules and official Fabric documentation.

    - Enroll in Microsoft training courses or instructor-led sessions if available.

CHAPTER 6   PRACTICE TESTS AND EXAM STRATEGIES

- Read through the latest Microsoft blogs and whitepapers on Fabric, Power BI, and data analytics.
- Follow Microsoft MVPs and community leaders for insights and tips.

5. **Join Study Groups and Communities**
   - Participate in LinkedIn groups, online forums, or Microsoft Tech Community discussions related to DP-600.
   - Engage in study groups to discuss complex topics and clear doubts with peers.
   - Attend webinars, AMA (Ask Me Anything) sessions, or meetups led by experts.

6. **Take Mock Exams**
   - Attempt full-length practice tests to assess your readiness.
   - Review incorrect answers to understand mistakes and reinforce learning.
   - Analyze performance trends across multiple mock exams and focus on weak areas.
   - Take scenario-based practice tests to improve critical thinking skills.

7. **Exam Day Strategies**
   - Get a good night's sleep before the exam to ensure focus and alertness.

- Arrive early if taking the test in a center or set up a distraction-free environment for an online proctored exam.
- Read each question carefully and avoid rushing to answer.
- Use the flagging option to revisit tricky questions later.
- Manage time efficiently, ensuring all questions are attempted before submission.

8. **Post-Exam Learning**
    - Regardless of the outcome, review areas where you struggled and continue learning.
    - Apply the knowledge gained in real-world projects to solidify your understanding.
    - If you pass, consider sharing your preparation journey and tips with the community.
    - If unsuccessful, review the score report, focus on weak areas, and reattempt with a refined strategy.

By following these strategies and consistently practicing, you can maximize your chances of passing the DP-600 certification exam with confidence!

ANNEXURE A

Key Concepts and Definitions

Microsoft Fabric Analytics Engineer Associate Certification

This glossary provides definitions for key concepts and terminologies relevant to the **Microsoft Fabric Analytics Engineer Associate** exam. It is structured to align with the exam objectives and essential knowledge areas required for certification.

1. Microsoft Fabric Overview

Microsoft Fabric
A unified, SaaS-based analytics platform that integrates multiple Microsoft data services, including Azure Synapse, Power BI, Data Factory, and OneLake.

OneLake
A single, unified data lake for Microsoft Fabric that acts as a storage layer across different Fabric workloads.

ANNEXURE A KEY CONCEPTS AND DEFINITIONS

Lakehouse Architecture

A hybrid model that combines the scalability of data lakes with the structured approach of data warehouses, enabling analytics and AI workloads.

Data Warehouse in Fabric

A high-performance, managed data warehouse service built on SQL-based architecture optimized for large-scale analytics.

Fabric Workloads

- **Data Engineering**: Large-scale data preparation, transformation, and processing
- **Data Science**: Machine learning model development and deployment
- **Data Warehousing**: Scalable SQL-based data storage and analytics
- **Real-Time Analytics**: Streaming and real-time data processing
- **Power BI**: Business intelligence reporting and visualization
- **Data Factory**: Orchestration and automation of data pipelines

Fabric Tenant and Capacity

- **Tenant**: A dedicated Microsoft Fabric environment associated with an organization
- **Capacity**: A subscription-based resource model for allocating compute and storage in Fabric

2. Data Preparation and Enrichment

Data Ingestion
The process of collecting and importing data from various sources into Microsoft Fabric, ensuring it is ready for analysis.

ETL (Extract, Transform, Load)
A traditional approach to data processing where data is extracted from sources, transformed into a suitable format, and then loaded into a data warehouse or lakehouse.

ELT (Extract, Load, Transform)
A modern approach where data is first loaded into a data storage system (e.g., a data lake) before transformation occurs. This is common in cloud-based analytics solutions.

Dataflows
A self-service data preparation tool in Power BI and Fabric that allows users to clean, transform, and enrich data before loading it into a semantic model.

Data Pipelines
A workflow used in Fabric to automate the movement, transformation, and processing of data across different services.

Data Transformation
The process of converting raw data into a structured format for analysis using tools like Power Query, Synapse Dataflows, and Data Factory pipelines.

   Data Wrangling vs. Data Cleaning

   - **Data Wrangling**: Preparing raw data for analysis, including reshaping and structuring
   - **Data Cleaning**: Identifying and correcting errors, inconsistencies, and missing values in datasets

ANNEXURE A KEY CONCEPTS AND DEFINITIONS

Delta Lake
An optimized storage layer for lakehouses that supports ACID transactions and schema enforcement.

Medallion Architecture (Bronze, Silver, Gold Layers)

- **Bronze Layer**: Raw, unprocessed data
- **Silver Layer**: Cleaned, enriched, and transformed data
- **Gold Layer**: Aggregated and business-ready data for reporting

3. Security and Maintenance of Analytical Assets

Row-Level Security (RLS)
A security feature that restricts access to data at the row level based on user roles.

Object-Level Security (OLS)
A security mechanism that controls access to entire tables or columns within a dataset.

Data Masking
A technique used to obscure sensitive information while maintaining data usability.

Azure Data Security and Governance
A set of security features (like Azure Purview and Microsoft Defender for Cloud) that help manage and protect analytics assets in Microsoft Fabric.

Data Sensitivity Labels
Security classifications applied to datasets to enforce compliance with data governance policies.

Data Access Control
Permissions and security settings that define who can read, modify, or manage datasets in Fabric.

Data Encryption
A security technique used to protect data at rest and in transit by converting it into unreadable formats.

Privileged Access Management (PAM)
A security approach that limits high-level permissions to prevent unauthorized data access.

Data Retention Policies
Rules that define how long data is stored and when it should be archived or deleted.

Microsoft Purview Integration
A governance tool that enables tracking of data lineage, classification, and compliance.

4. Implementing and Managing Semantic Models

Semantic Model
A structured data model used in Power BI and Fabric that allows users to build relationships, calculations, and aggregations for business intelligence reporting.

Power BI Dataset
A type of semantic model that stores imported data or connects live to external data sources for analysis.

DirectQuery Mode
A connection method that allows Power BI reports to query data directly from the source without importing it.

ANNEXURE A   KEY CONCEPTS AND DEFINITIONS

Composite Models
A feature in Power BI that enables combining multiple data sources in a single dataset, using both DirectQuery and Import modes.

Aggregation Tables
Precomputed summary tables used in semantic models to optimize query performance.

Import Mode vs. DirectQuery vs. Hybrid Mode

- **Import Mode**: Data is fully loaded into Power BI for fast performance.
- **DirectQuery**: Live queries are sent to the data source without importing data.
- **Hybrid Mode**: A mix of Import and DirectQuery for optimized performance.

Measure vs. Calculated Column vs. Calculated Table

- **Measure**: A dynamic calculation performed in reports (e.g., SUM, AVERAGE)
- **Calculated Column**: A computed field added to a table during data modeling
- **Calculated Table**: A new table derived from an existing dataset using DAX

Fact Table vs. Dimension Table

- **Fact Table**: Contains transactional data (e.g., sales, revenue)
- **Dimension Table**: Contains descriptive data (e.g., customers, products)

Star Schema vs. Snowflake Schema

- **Star Schema**: A simple data model with fact tables connected to multiple dimension tables

- **Snowflake Schema**: A normalized schema with dimension tables further split into sub-dimensions

Aggregation Strategy

A technique used to precompute summaries of large datasets for performance optimization.

Composite Models and Dual Mode Storage

A Power BI feature that allows users to combine different data connectivity modes within a single model.

5. Querying and Analyzing Data

Structured Query Language (SQL)

A programming language used to manage and query relational databases.

Kusto Query Language (KQL)

A query language used in Azure Data Explorer and Microsoft Fabric for analyzing large volumes of structured and semi-structured data.

Data Analysis Expressions (DAX)

A formula language used in Power BI and semantic models for creating custom calculations, measures, and aggregations.

Common Table Expressions (CTEs)

A SQL feature that simplifies complex queries by allowing the creation of temporary result sets.

ANNEXURE A   KEY CONCEPTS AND DEFINITIONS

Window Functions (SQL & DAX)

Functions that allow calculations across a specified range of rows within a query result, useful for running totals, moving averages, and ranking.

SQL Joins

- **INNER JOIN**: Returns only matching records from both tables
- **LEFT JOIN**: Returns all records from the left table and matching records from the right table
- **RIGHT JOIN**: Returns all records from the right table and matching records from the left table
- **FULL JOIN**: Returns all records from both tables, filling in NULLs where there is no match

SQL vs. KQL vs. DAX

Feature	SQL	KQL	DAX
Usage	Relational databases	Big data analytics	Power BI and semantic models
Syntax	Standard SQL	Schema-free, optimized for logs	Function-based, optimized for BI
Example Query	SELECT * FROM Sales	Sales	Take 100

DAX Time Intelligence Functions

- **TOTALYTD()**: Year-to-date total
- **PARALLELPERIOD()**: Compares data from different time periods
- **DATESINPERIOD()**: Returns a range of dates based on a given interval

KQL Operators

- **where**: Filters data
- **summarize**: Aggregates data
- **project**: Selects specific columns
- **extend**: Creates calculated columns

Performance Optimization Techniques

- **Partitioning large tables** for better query performance
- **Using materialized views** to precompute complex queries
- **Applying indexing strategies** for efficient lookups

6. Stakeholder Collaboration and Best Practices

Business Intelligence (BI)
A set of processes and technologies used to transform raw data into meaningful insights for decision-making.

Data Governance
The management of data availability, integrity, and security to ensure compliance with organizational and regulatory requirements.

Data Lineage
A visualization of how data moves and transforms within an organization's data ecosystem, ensuring transparency and traceability.

Self-Service Analytics
A framework that enables business users to create reports and dashboards independently using tools like Power BI and Microsoft Fabric.

ANNEXURE A   KEY CONCEPTS AND DEFINITIONS

Data Fabric vs. Data Lake vs. Data Warehouse

- **Data Fabric**: A unified architecture that integrates various data sources, ensuring seamless data management and governance

- **Data Lake**: A storage repository that holds raw, unstructured, and structured data at scale

- **Data Warehouse**: A structured database optimized for fast querying and reporting

Microsoft OneLake Shortcuts

A feature that allows linking external storage locations (e.g., AWS S3, ADLS) into Fabric.

CI/CD for Power BI and Fabric

Using DevOps pipelines for version control, testing, and deployment of reports and datasets.

Power BI Dataflows vs. Fabric Data Pipelines

- **Dataflows**: Self-service data preparation in Power BI

- **Data Pipelines**: Enterprise-grade ETL/ELT workflows in Fabric

7. Real-Time Analytics and Monitoring

Event Stream Processing

A technique used in Fabric to analyze streaming data from IoT devices, logs, and real-time applications.

Azure Stream Analytics vs. Kusto Engine

- **Azure Stream Analytics**: Processes real-time streaming data.
- **Kusto Engine**: Optimized for ad hoc querying of large log data.

Push vs. Scheduled Data Refresh

- **Push Refresh**: Data is updated in real time when changes occur.
- **Scheduled Refresh**: Data is updated at predefined intervals.

Conclusion

This annexure serves as a quick reference guide to essential **Microsoft Fabric** concepts. It ensures clarity on exam-related topics, helping candidates reinforce their knowledge and succeed in the **Fabric Analytics Engineer Associate Certification**.

ANNEXURE B

Common Interview Questions and Answers

This annexure provides a collection of common interview questions that aspiring Microsoft Fabric Analytics Engineers may encounter. These questions cover key concepts, practical applications, and problem-solving scenarios related to Microsoft Fabric and analytics engineering.

1. **Microsoft Fabric Fundamentals**

    Q1: What is Microsoft Fabric, and how does it differ from traditional analytics platforms?

    A: Microsoft Fabric is a **unified analytics platform** integrating **data engineering, data science, data warehousing, and real-time analytics** under a single ecosystem. Unlike traditional analytics platforms that require separate services, Fabric consolidates functionalities from **Azure Synapse, Power BI, Data Factory, and OneLake**, providing a seamless experience.

Q2: What are the key components of Microsoft Fabric?

A: The key components include

- **OneLake**: Unified data lake for all workloads
- **Data Engineering**: ETL and data transformation
- **Data Science**: AI/ML model training and deployment
- **Data Warehousing**: Managed SQL-based data warehouse
- **Real-Time Analytics**: Streaming and log data processing
- **Power BI**: Reporting and visualization
- **Data Factory**: Data pipeline orchestration

2. **Data Preparation and ETL**

Q3: How do you prepare raw data for analytics in Fabric?

A:

- Use **Dataflows** or **Data Pipelines** for ETL processes.
- Apply **data transformation techniques** (filtering, cleaning, aggregating).
- Use **Medallion Architecture** (Bronze-Silver-Gold layers) for structured data processing.
- Store cleaned data in **OneLake or a Fabric Warehouse** for analysis.

Q4: What is the difference between Dataflows and Data Pipelines in Fabric?

A:

- **Dataflows**: Power BI-based self-service ETL tool
- **Data Pipelines**: Enterprise-grade **orchestrated ETL/ELT** workflows in Fabric (similar to Azure Data Factory)

3. **Data Security and Governance**

Q5: How do you implement data security in Fabric?

A:

- **Row-Level Security (RLS)** to restrict access to specific rows
- **Sensitivity Labels** for data classification
- **Role-Based Access Control (RBAC)** to manage permissions
- **Encryption** for data protection at rest and in transit
- **Microsoft Purview Integration** for compliance and data lineage tracking

Q6: What is Row-Level Security (RLS), and how does it work in Power BI?

A:

RLS restricts data access at the **row level** based on user roles. It is implemented by

- Defining **roles** in **Power BI Desktop** using **DAX expressions**
- Assigning roles to users in **Power BI Service**

Example DAX filter for RLS:

```
[Region] = USERPRINCIPALNAME()
```

This ensures that users can only see data for their assigned **Region**.

4. **Data Modeling and Semantic Layers**

Q7: Explain the difference between Import Mode and DirectQuery in Power BI.

A:

Mode	Description	Performance	Data Refresh
Import	Loads data into Power BI	Faster	Needs periodic refresh
DirectQuery	Queries data in real-time from the source	Slower	No refresh needed
Hybrid	Uses a combination of both	Optimized	Supports real-time and batch data

Q8: What is a Star Schema, and why is it preferred for analytical workloads?

A:

A **Star Schema** is a database design where a **central fact table** is linked to multiple **dimension tables**. It is preferred because

- **Improves query performance** by reducing joins
- **Simplifies reporting** by organizing data logically
- **Optimized for aggregations** in Power BI and Fabric

Example:

- **Fact Table**: Sales (Transaction ID, Product ID, Amount, Date)
- **Dimension Tables**: Products, Customers, Date, Region

5. **Querying and Analyzing Data**

Q9: How do you optimize SQL queries for large datasets in Fabric?

A:

- **Use indexing** on frequently queried columns.
- **Apply partitioning** to large tables.
- **Leverage materialized views** for precomputed aggregations.
- **Use efficient joins** and avoid unnecessary subqueries.

ANNEXURE B COMMON INTERVIEW QUESTIONS AND ANSWERS

Q10: What are the key differences between SQL, KQL, and DAX?

A:

Feature	SQL	KQL	DAX
Usage	Relational databases	Log and real-time analytics	Power BI semantic models
Syntax	Standard SQL	Schema-free	Function-based
Example	SELECT * FROM Sales	Sales	Take 100

6. **Real-Time Analytics**

Q11: How does Fabric handle real-time data processing?

A: Fabric supports real-time analytics through

- **Kusto Engine** for large-scale streaming data analysis
- **Event Streams** for IoT and log processing
- **Direct Lake Mode** for real-time reporting in Power BI

Q12: What are Push and Scheduled Refresh in Power BI?

A:

- **Push Refresh**: Updates data in real-time when changes occur
- **Scheduled Refresh**: Refreshes data at predefined intervals (e.g., hourly, daily)

ANNEXURE B COMMON INTERVIEW QUESTIONS AND ANSWERS

7. **Performance Optimization and Deployment**

Q13: How do you improve Power BI report performance?

A:

- **Use Aggregations** to precompute summaries.
- **Optimize DAX measures** to reduce computation time.
- **Enable Query Reduction settings** to limit data queries.
- **Use Composite Models** to balance performance and data freshness.

Q14: What is Continuous Integration and Deployment (CI/CD) in Fabric?

A:

CI/CD automates report development and deployment using **Azure DevOps** and **GitHub Actions**. It ensures

- Version control of Power BI reports and datasets
- Automated testing of data models
- Streamlined deployment across environments (Dev ➤ Test ➤ Prod)

8. **Scenario-Based Questions**

Q15: A stakeholder reports slow performance on a Power BI report. How do you troubleshoot?

A: Steps to troubleshoot:

ANNEXURE B   COMMON INTERVIEW QUESTIONS AND ANSWERS

1. **Check query performance** (slow SQL/KQL queries).
2. **Reduce data volume** (filter unnecessary records).
3. **Optimize DAX calculations** (avoid complex nested functions).
4. **Review data model schema** (Star Schema vs. Snowflake).
5. **Enable Aggregations and Indexing** in Fabric.

Q16: Your organization wants to migrate from an on-prem SQL Server to Microsoft Fabric. What steps would you take?

A:

1. **Assess existing data sources** and dependencies.
2. **Choose the appropriate Fabric workload** (Warehouse, Lakehouse).
3. **Use Data Pipelines** to migrate and transform data.
4. **Implement governance policies** (RLS, sensitivity labels).
5. **Optimize performance** using indexing and partitioning.

9. **Microsoft Fabric Advanced Concepts**

Q17: What is OneSecurity in Microsoft Fabric, and why is it important?

A:

OneSecurity is Fabric's unified security model across all workloads (Data Engineering, Warehousing, Real-Time Analytics, etc.). It ensures consistent permission management and data protection policies, reducing complexity and ensuring compliance across the platform.

Q18: Explain the concept of Direct Lake in Power BI and how it differs from Import Mode and DirectQuery.

A:

Direct Lake allows Power BI to access data directly from OneLake storage without copying it into a dataset or querying a live source. It combines the best of Import (speed) and DirectQuery (freshness) modes, enabling fast real-time analysis on large datasets without data duplication.

10. **Fabric Workloads and Use Cases**

    Q19: When would you choose a Lakehouse vs. a Warehouse in Microsoft Fabric?

    A:

    - **Lakehouse:** Best for unstructured/semi-structured data and big data analytics with open data formats like Delta Lake
    - **Warehouse:** Best for structured data and traditional business intelligence scenarios requiring SQL-based management

ANNEXURE B COMMON INTERVIEW QUESTIONS AND ANSWERS

Q20: What is the role of Notebooks in Fabric, and when would you use them?

A:

Notebooks in Fabric (similar to Synapse and Databricks) allow users to run code (Python, SQL, Spark) interactively for data exploration, transformation, and machine learning. They are ideal for advanced data prep, model training, and exploratory analytics.

11. **Machine Learning Integration**

Q21: How can you build and deploy machine learning models within Microsoft Fabric?

A:

- Use the **Data Science** workload in Fabric with integrated notebooks.
- Train models using libraries like scikit-learn, PySpark MLlib, or Azure ML integration.
- Deploy models as endpoints for scoring or integrate predictions into data pipelines or Power BI reports.

12. **Monitoring and Cost Management**

Q22: How do you monitor resource usage and optimize costs in Microsoft Fabric?

A:

- Use the Fabric Monitoring Hub for workload performance and resource consumption insights.

- Set budgets and alerts via Azure Cost Management.
- Optimize query efficiency, leverage Auto-Pause for inactive compute resources, and use reserved capacity options.

13. **Troubleshooting**

Q23: A data pipeline in Fabric fails intermittently. How would you troubleshoot it?

A:

- Check activity logs for errors.
- Validate source and destination connectivity.
- Examine data transformation steps for bad data or schema mismatches.
- Implement retry policies for transient failures.

14. **Power BI Specifics**

Q24: What is the advantage of using Field Parameters in Power BI?

A:

Field Parameters allow users to dynamically change dimensions or measures used in visuals without altering the underlying model, enhancing report interactivity without writing complex DAX.

Q25: How do Aggregations help in scaling big datasets in Power BI with Fabric?

A:

Aggregations precompute summary data at different levels. Power BI intelligently switches between detailed and aggregated tables based on query granularity, significantly improving performance on large datasets.

15. **Fabric Architecture and Integration**

Q26: How does Microsoft Fabric integrate with Azure services like Synapse, Azure ML, and Data Factory?

A:

Fabric inherits and integrates functionalities from these services:

- **Synapse** (analytics engine for SQL & Spark)
- **Azure ML** (for machine learning integration)
- **Data Factory** (for pipeline orchestration)

    Fabric provides a *single SaaS platform* where these capabilities are unified without managing separate infrastructures.

Q27: What is the importance of Open Data Formats (like Delta Lake) in Fabric?

ANNEXURE B   COMMON INTERVIEW QUESTIONS AND ANSWERS

A:

Open formats ensure data interoperability across tools and platforms. Delta Lake provides ACID transactions, time travel, and scalable metadata handling, making it ideal for analytics and machine learning workflows.

16. **Fabric Administration and Best Practices**

    Q28: How would you manage workspace organization in Fabric for a large enterprise?

    A:

    - Create workspaces per department, project, or environment (Dev/Test/Prod).
    - Apply Role-Based Access Control (RBAC) at the workspace level.
    - Use naming conventions and tagging.
    - Automate workspace creation via APIs if needed.

    Q29: What are Fabric capacities, and how do they affect performance and cost?

    A:

    Capacities are reserved compute and storage units in Fabric. Higher capacities (SKU levels) offer more resources for faster query execution, more concurrency, and bigger datasets, but also increase costs.

17. **Data Governance Deep Dive**

    Q30: How does Microsoft Purview enhance data governance in Fabric?

    A:

    Purview provides a centralized catalog, automated data lineage tracking, sensitivity label propagation, and compliance reporting. It helps organizations meet data privacy laws like GDPR while maintaining audit trails.

18. **Advanced Data Modeling**

    Q31: What are Calculation Groups in Power BI, and why are they important?

    A:

    Calculation Groups allow the creation of reusable DAX expressions (like time intelligence functions) without duplicating measures. They simplify models, improve maintainability, and reduce the number of measures needed.

    Q32: What is a Composite Model in Power BI, and when would you use it?

    A:

    Composite Models allow combining Import and DirectQuery data sources in the same report. Useful when some data needs real-time updates while others can be cached for performance.

ANNEXURE B COMMON INTERVIEW QUESTIONS AND ANSWERS

19. **Fabric Real-Time Advanced Concepts**

    Q33: What is the role of Eventstream in Microsoft Fabric?

    A:

    Eventstream ingests and processes real-time data streams (from IoT devices, logs, apps) with transformations before sending it to storage (OneLake), Real-Time Analytics databases, or Power BI dashboards.

20. **Deployment and Automation**

    Q34: How would you automate dataset refreshes and deployment pipelines in Fabric?

    A:

    - Use Git Integration for version control.
    - Set up deployment pipelines (Dev/Test/Prod).
    - Use REST APIs for automation (like triggering dataset refreshes).
    - Integrate CI/CD with Azure DevOps or GitHub Actions.

21. **Scenario-Based Critical Thinking**

    Q35: How would you design an architecture for handling both batch and real-time data in Fabric?

    A:

    - **Batch:** Use Data Pipelines + Lakehouse/Warehouse.

- **Real-Time:** Use Eventstream + Real-Time Analytics databases.
- Connect both into OneLake for unified storage.
- Build semantic models in Power BI that query both sources appropriately.

Q36: A Fabric report is failing to refresh due to large dataset size. What would you do?

A:

- Reduce dataset size via aggregations.
- Use Incremental Refresh.
- Review data model (star schema).
- Split datasets if necessary.
- Upgrade capacity or optimize queries.

22. **Career and Soft Skills Questions**

Q37: How do you stay updated with new features in Microsoft Fabric and Power BI?

A:

Examples include following Microsoft Fabric blog, joining the Fabric Community, attending webinars, participating in preview programs, and reading Microsoft Learn content.

Q38: Tell us about a challenging Fabric or Power BI project you worked on. What was your approach and outcome?

(*This is an open-ended storytelling question for senior candidates.*)

Q39: How would you explain the value of Microsoft Fabric to a non-technical stakeholder?

A:

Use simple language—explain that Fabric combines all the necessary tools (data storage, analysis, reporting) into one platform, saving time, cost, and effort. Highlight business benefits like faster decision-making and better data governance.

Q40: How do you prioritize tasks when handling multiple Fabric projects simultaneously?

A:

- Assess business impact and deadlines.
- Break down tasks using Agile/Scrum methods.
- Communicate regularly with stakeholders about progress and blockers.
- Use tools like Azure DevOps or Trello for task management.

Q41: If you are given a Fabric tool you've never used before, how would you approach learning it?

A:

- Start with Microsoft Learn modules.
- Explore official documentation and tutorials.
- Experiment in a sandbox environment.
- Join communities/forums for best practices.
- Apply learning to a mini-project.

Q42: Describe a time when a Power BI or Fabric report did not meet stakeholder expectations. How did you handle it?

(*Behavioral question.*)

A:

- Listen carefully to feedback without being defensive.
- Understand the gap between expectations and delivery.
- Quickly propose adjustments or a phased improvement plan.
- Keep communication open until the stakeholder is satisfied.

Q43: What strategies do you use to communicate technical challenges to nontechnical users?

A:

- Avoid jargon; use analogies or simple examples.
- Focus on the *impact* rather than technical details.
- Offer visual aids (diagrams, simplified workflows).
- Ensure two-way communication to confirm understanding.

ANNEXURE B   COMMON INTERVIEW QUESTIONS AND ANSWERS

Q44: How do you ensure collaboration when working with cross-functional teams (e.g., data engineers, analysts, business users)?

A:

- Hold regular stand-ups or check-ins.
- Use clear documentation and shared repositories.
- Set common goals and deliverables.
- Respect different perspectives and expertise.

Q45: What motivates you to work in data analytics and platforms like Microsoft Fabric?

(*Personal values and passion check.*)

A:

Sample answer:

"I enjoy transforming raw data into meaningful insights that drive real-world business decisions. Platforms like Fabric amplify this impact by making complex processes simpler and more powerful."

Q46: If you had to mentor a junior Fabric Analytics Engineer, what would your first lesson be?

A:

Teach the importance of understanding the business problem before jumping into technical solutions—data without context is just noise.

Q47: How do you balance innovation (trying new features/tools) versus stability (keeping systems reliable)?

A:

- Use Proof of Concepts (POCs) to test new features safely.
- Gradually roll out changes after thorough testing.
- Keep production environments stable while experimenting in separate environments.

Q48: How do you handle feedback or criticism on your work, especially in a high-pressure project?

A:

- View feedback as an opportunity to improve.
- Remain calm and ask clarifying questions if needed.
- Apply constructive feedback quickly to show responsiveness.

More General Interview Questions for Microsoft Fabric Analytics Engineer

Understanding and Analytical Thinking

Q49: How do you approach solving a data problem when requirements are unclear?

ANNEXURE B   COMMON INTERVIEW QUESTIONS AND ANSWERS

A:

- Ask clarifying questions to stakeholders.
- Break down the problem into smaller parts.
- Create a prototype and iterate based on feedback.

Q50: Can you explain a technical concept you recently learned to me like I'm a beginner?

(*Tests communication and understanding skills.*)

Q51: Give an example where you had to learn a new technology quickly for a project. How did you manage it?

Sample Answer:

Situation:

In one of my previous roles, we were transitioning our data processing pipelines from traditional ETL tools to Microsoft Fabric. I had limited prior experience with Fabric, and the project timeline was aggressive.

Task:

I was responsible for designing the new data ingestion and transformation pipelines using Fabric's Data Engineering capabilities within just a few weeks.

Action

- I immediately **created a focused learning plan** by identifying key features I needed to master — like Data Pipelines, OneLake, and Lakehouses.
- I spent the first few days completing **official Microsoft documentation, learning paths, and hands-on labs**.
- I also **joined Fabric community forums** and **attended webinars** to stay updated with real-world use cases and best practices.

- For efficient learning, I applied a **"learn by doing"** approach—building small pilot projects in a sandbox environment while studying.

- I maintained a **running list of challenges and solutions** to avoid repeating mistakes and to help the team later.

- Finally, I **collaborated closely with experts**—reaching out to a Microsoft-certified trainer for a couple of quick consultation sessions.

Result

Within two weeks, I was able to design and deliver the initial phase of the pipelines. Not only was the project completed on time, but I also shared my learning resources and best practices internally, helping **speed up the learning curve** for the rest of the team.

Adaptability and Problem-Solving

Q52: Microsoft Fabric is evolving fast. How do you stay updated with the latest features and changes?

A:

- Follow Microsoft Learn, Tech Community, blogs.
- Attend Fabric webinars and Fabric Community Calls.
- Experiment regularly with new preview features.

Q53: Have you ever disagreed with a team member on a technical decision? How did you resolve it?

A:

- Focused on facts and data, not opinions.
- Suggested a Proof of Concept (POC) to test ideas.
- Prioritized the project's goals over personal views.

ANNEXURE B   COMMON INTERVIEW QUESTIONS AND ANSWERS

Customer Focus and Business Impact

Q54: How would you measure the success of a Power BI dashboard or a Fabric data solution?

A:

- Adoption rate (are users using it?).
- Business outcomes (improved decision-making, faster processes).
- User feedback and satisfaction.
- Performance metrics (query speed, data freshness).

Q55: What business KPIs (Key Performance Indicators) would you track when working on a Fabric analytics project for an e-commerce company?

Teamwork and Leadership

Q56: How do you balance independent work and collaboration when building analytics solutions?

A:

- Start with team discussions to align expectations.
- Work independently but schedule regular checkpoints.
- Share progress early to gather feedback.

Q57: Describe a time when you had to train or guide nontechnical users on using Power BI/Fabric reports. How did you ensure they understood?

Sample Answer:

Situation

At my previous company, we launched a new set of Power BI dashboards for the Sales and Marketing team. However, many users were nontechnical and unfamiliar with how to interact with reports or interpret the visualizations.

ANNEXURE B   COMMON INTERVIEW QUESTIONS AND ANSWERS

Task

My task was to train the team so they could confidently use the dashboards for daily decision-making without depending on IT support.

Action

- I first organized short **hands-on workshops**, each focused on a specific dashboard—keeping it simple and scenario-based.

- I avoided technical jargon and instead explained concepts using **business language**—for example, I referred to filters as "choosing your region" rather than explaining slicers.

- I created **simple one-page guides** with screenshots showing steps like "How to filter data" and "How to export a report to Excel."

- During the sessions, I encouraged **live practice**, where users performed tasks themselves instead of just watching me.

- I also scheduled a **follow-up "office hours"** session for 1-on-1 support if anyone needed extra help.

Result

The team quickly became confident in using the reports. Adoption rates increased by **40% within the first month**, and the Sales team reported making faster, more informed decisions based on the insights they gathered themselves without IT intervention.

ANNEXURE B   COMMON INTERVIEW QUESTIONS AND ANSWERS

Detailed Interview Tips for Microsoft Fabric Analytics Engineers

1. **Preparation Tips**

    - **Know Microsoft Fabric Inside Out**: Review all workloads—Data Engineering, Data Warehousing, Real-Time Analytics, OneLake, Data Factory, Power BI.

    - **Understand Integration Points**: Like how Fabric works with Purview, Azure DevOps, GitHub.

    - **Learn About Medallion Architecture**: Bronze, Silver, Gold layers—this often comes up!

    - **Be Ready for Scenario-Based Questions**: They will ask about real-world challenges like "What if the data pipeline fails?" or "How to optimize a slow dashboard?"

2. **Communication Tips**

    - **Use the STAR technique** for behavioral questions:

        Situation ➤ Task ➤ Action ➤ Result.

        (It gives your answers structure and shows clear thinking.)

    - **Speak in business language when needed**: Focus not just on *how* you solved something technically, but *why* it mattered for the business.

3. **Technical Demonstration Tips**

    - **Be Ready for Live Exercises**: They may ask you to build a small Dataflow, create a simple Power BI report, or write a basic SQL/KQL query.

    - **Explain Your Thought Process**: Even if you get stuck, show how you are thinking logically—it matters more than the exact answer sometimes.

4. **Soft Skills Tips**

    - **Show Curiosity and Humility**:

    ("I'm excited to continuously learn Fabric's evolving features and apply them effectively.")

    - **Ask Smart Questions at the End**:

    Example: "How does your team leverage Real-Time Analytics inside Microsoft Fabric for business-critical workflows?"

5. **Bonus: Best First Impression Practices**

    - **Arrive early** (if virtual, log in 5–10 minutes early).

    - **Dress neatly but smart-casual** (for tech interviews, formal is not usually required unless explicitly stated).

    - **Smile and be positive**—show energy and passion for analytics work!

    - **Carry a notepad**—jot down key points if needed (even in virtual interviews).

Conclusion

This annexure provides a solid foundation for interview preparation, covering both theoretical and practical aspects of Microsoft Fabric Analytics Engineering. Mastering these topics will help candidates confidently tackle real-world interview scenarios.

ANNEXURE C

Microsoft Fabric – Specific Keyboard Shortcuts

General Microsoft Fabric Shortcuts

Action	Shortcut
Open OneLake	Ctrl + O
Open Data Pipeline	Alt + P
Open Notebook	Ctrl + Shift + N
Refresh Power BI Report	F5
Open Settings	Ctrl + ,
Toggle Full Screen	F11
Open Help	F1

ANNEXURE C   MICROSOFT FABRIC – SPECIFIC KEYBOARD SHORTCUTS

Power BI and Data Modeling Shortcuts

Action	Shortcut
Open Data Model	Ctrl + M
Open SQL Query Editor	Ctrl + Shift + E
Run SQL Query	Ctrl + Enter
Refresh Dataset	Ctrl + R
Show/Hide Fields Pane	Ctrl + F
Show/Hide Filters Pane	Ctrl + Shift + F
Show/Hide Visualizations Pane	Ctrl + Shift + V
Create New Report	Ctrl + N

DAX Query Shortcuts

Action	Shortcut
Open DAX Query Editor	Ctrl + Shift + D
Evaluate DAX Query	F5
Format DAX Code	Ctrl + Shift + F

SQL Query Editor Shortcuts

Action	Shortcut
Open SQL Query Editor	Ctrl + Shift + E
Run SQL Query	Ctrl + Enter
Format SQL Code	Ctrl + Shift + F
Comment/Uncomment Code	Ctrl + /
Find and Replace	Ctrl + H

Kusto Query Language (KQL) Shortcuts

Action	Shortcut
Open KQL Query Editor	Ctrl + K
Run KQL Query	Shift + Enter
Format KQL Code	Ctrl + Shift + F
Toggle Comments	Ctrl + /
Find in Query	Ctrl + F

Data Pipelines and OneLake Shortcuts

Action	Shortcut
Run Data Pipeline	Ctrl + Shift + P
Open Lakehouse Explorer	Ctrl + L
Upload File to OneLake	Ctrl + U
Refresh Lakehouse View	F5

ANNEXURE C   MICROSOFT FABRIC – SPECIFIC KEYBOARD SHORTCUTS

Notebooks and Python/ML Shortcuts

Action	Shortcut
Run Notebook Cell	Shift + Enter
Insert New Cell	Alt + Enter
Delete Current Cell	D D (Press 'D' twice)
Toggle Cell Type (Code/Markdown)	M for Markdown, Y for Code
Run All Cells	Ctrl + Shift + Enter
Restart Kernel	Ctrl + .

ANNEXURE D

Case Studies and Real-World Scenarios

Practical use cases of Microsoft Fabric in different industries.

Microsoft Fabric is revolutionizing data analytics by integrating **OneLake, Synapse Data Warehouses, Power BI, and AI-driven models** into a single analytics ecosystem. Below are five **real-world case studies** demonstrating how Fabric can solve industry-specific challenges.

1. Healthcare: Predictive Analytics for Patient Readmission

Scenario

A large hospital network noticed an **increase in patient readmission rates** within 30 days of discharge. This was affecting hospital efficiency, increasing operational costs, and leading to penalties from insurance providers. The hospital needed a solution to identify **high-risk patients** and **intervene early** to prevent unnecessary readmissions.

- **Fabric Solution:**
    - **Data Sources**
        - Electronic Health Records (EHR) from hospital databases

- IoT data from patient monitoring devices (heart rate, blood pressure, glucose levels)
- Pharmacy prescription records
- Insurance claims and past admission history

- **Implementation**
  - All data was **ingested into OneLake** to provide a centralized data repository.
  - A **Synapse Data Warehouse** stored structured patient records.
  - Machine learning models in **Azure Machine Learning** analyzed patterns in patient readmission.
  - A **Power BI Dashboard** visualized patients at high risk of readmission, helping doctors make proactive decisions.
  - Automated alerts were sent via **Power Automate** to medical teams when a high-risk patient was discharged.

Impact

✓ Readmission rates reduced by **20%** with early intervention strategies.

✓ Doctors could prioritize care for high-risk patients based on **real-time risk scores**.

✓ Insurance penalties were reduced, saving the hospital millions in fines.

ANNEXURE D   CASE STUDIES AND REAL-WORLD SCENARIOS

2. Retail: Demand Forecasting for Inventory Optimization

Scenario

A multinational retail chain was struggling with **stock shortages and overstocking** during seasonal sales. Without **accurate demand forecasting**, some stores experienced **out-of-stock issues**, while others had excess inventory leading to markdowns and revenue loss.

Fabric Solution:

- **Data Sources**
  - Point of Sale (POS) data from retail stores
  - Customer purchase history and loyalty program data
  - External data sources: weather forecasts, social media trends

- **Implementation**
  - All data was streamed into **Microsoft Fabric Data Pipelines** to **OneLake**.
  - A **Lakehouse** architecture allowed integration of structured and unstructured data.
  - **AutoML models** analyzed demand patterns based on customer behavior and external trends.
  - A **Power BI Dashboard** provided real-time insights to supply chain managers.
  - Stores received **automated restocking recommendations** based on AI-driven forecasts.

Impact

- ✓ Increased revenue by **15%** by stocking in-demand products.
- ✓ Reduced product wastage by **30%** through precise inventory management.
- ✓ Improved customer satisfaction by ensuring availability of popular products.

3. Finance: Fraud Detection in Credit Card Transactions

Scenario
A global bank was experiencing **rising fraud cases** in online transactions. Traditional fraud detection systems were **slow** and **reactive**, leading to significant financial losses and customer dissatisfaction.

Fabric Solution:

- **Data Sources**
  - Credit card transaction logs
  - Customer spending behavior and profile data
  - Location and IP tracking data
- **Implementation**
  - Transaction data was streamed into **KQL Databases** in Microsoft Fabric for real-time analytics.
  - **Anomaly detection models** built in **Azure Machine Learning** flagged suspicious transactions.

- A **KQL query-based alert system** detected deviations in spending behavior.

- **Power BI Reports** helped fraud analysts monitor fraud trends.

- Automated workflows in **Power Automate** triggered alerts when fraud was detected.

Impact

✓ **40% faster detection** of fraudulent transactions.

✓ Reduced financial losses due to fraud by millions annually.

✓ Improved customer trust and security in online banking.

4. Manufacturing: IoT-Based Predictive Maintenance

Scenario

A manufacturing company faced frequent **machine breakdowns**, leading to **production delays and high maintenance costs.** The company wanted a **predictive maintenance** system to detect machine failures before they happened.

Fabric Solution:

- **Data Sources**
  - IoT sensors tracking machine temperature, vibration, and performance
  - Historical maintenance logs
  - Production line efficiency metrics

- **Implementation**
  - **Azure Event Hub** collected **real-time IoT sensor data** and streamed it into **OneLake**.
  - A **Time-Series Database** stored historical machine performance data.
  - **KQL queries** analyzed trends to detect early signs of failure.
  - **Power BI Dashboards** displayed machine health scores for plant managers.
  - Anomaly detection algorithms sent **real-time alerts to maintenance teams**.

Impact

- ✓ Machine downtime reduced by **35%** due to proactive repairs.
- ✓ Annual maintenance cost savings of over **$2 million**.
- ✓ Increased **operational efficiency** with predictive maintenance scheduling.

5. Government: Smart City Traffic Optimization

Scenario

A city government wanted to reduce **traffic congestion and pollution** by analyzing **real-time traffic flow data** and adjusting traffic signals dynamically.

Fabric Solution:

- **Data Sources**
  - GPS and traffic sensor data from city roads
  - CCTV footage and vehicle detection AI models
  - Weather conditions affecting traffic flow

- **Implementation**
  - **Streaming Dataflows** ingested live GPS and IoT sensor data into **OneLake**.
  - **Geospatial Analysis using KQL** detected congestion hotspots.
  - AI-powered **traffic signal optimization** adjusted light durations dynamically.
  - A **Power BI Dashboard** provided real-time monitoring for city planners.
  - **Power Automate** sent alerts to drivers via navigation apps when roads were congested.

Impact

- ✓ **25% reduction** in traffic congestion during peak hours.
- ✓ **10% decrease** in vehicle emissions due to optimized traffic flow.
- ✓ Improved **public transport efficiency** by prioritizing bus lanes dynamically.

ANNEXURE D   CASE STUDIES AND REAL-WORLD SCENARIOS

6. Education: AI-Powered Student Performance Prediction

Scenario

A university wanted to **identify at-risk students** early and provide personalized learning support to improve graduation rates.

- **Fabric Solution:**

    - **Data Sources**

        - Student attendance records

        - Exam scores and assignment submissions

        - Learning management system (LMS) interaction data

        - Socioeconomic background data

    - **Implementation**

        - **Data collected from multiple LMS platforms** was stored in **OneLake**.

        - A **Synapse Data Warehouse** structured historical academic data.

        - AI-based **predictive models** identified students at risk of failing courses.

        - **Power BI Dashboards** provided faculty with real-time academic insights.

        - Personalized learning recommendations were sent to students via **Power Automate notifications**.

Impact

- ✓ **Graduation rates improved by 15%** with early intervention.
- ✓ Professors could **identify struggling students** faster and offer support.
- ✓ Adaptive learning strategies helped **personalize coursework**.

7. Energy: Smart Grid Energy Consumption Optimization

Scenario

An energy provider needed to **optimize electricity distribution** based on real-time demand and prevent **blackouts** during peak hours.

Fabric Solution:

- **Data Sources**
  - Smart meters from homes and businesses
  - Weather data affecting energy consumption
  - Historical power usage patterns
- **Implementation**
  - Smart meter readings were **streamed into OneLake via Data Pipelines**.
  - A **Synapse Data Warehouse** stored structured customer energy consumption data.
  - **Machine learning models** forecasted energy demand spikes.

- **KQL queries** detected anomalies in power consumption, preventing outages.
- **Power BI Dashboards** displayed real-time electricity demand insights for grid operators.

Impact

- ✓ **Power grid efficiency increased by 25%** due to real-time energy redistribution.
- ✓ Reduced **blackouts and power losses** during peak usage hours.
- ✓ **Lowered electricity costs** by optimizing supply based on predictive demand.

8. Telecom: Customer Churn Reduction with AI Insights

Scenario

A telecom company was experiencing **high customer churn rates** and needed a **data-driven strategy** to retain subscribers.

Fabric Solution:

- **Data Sources**
    - Call drop frequency and network performance data
    - Customer complaints and support call logs
    - Subscription renewal and payment data
    - Social media sentiment analysis

ANNEXURE D   CASE STUDIES AND REAL-WORLD SCENARIOS

- **Implementation**
  - **Fabric Data Pipelines** ingested real-time customer interactions.
  - A **Synapse Data Warehouse** stored structured churn risk data.
  - **AI models identified high-risk customers** likely to leave based on usage patterns.
  - **Sentiment analysis** on social media tracked negative feedback.
  - **Power BI Dashboards** provided customer service teams with insights to offer targeted discounts.
  - **Power Automate** sent retention offers to high-risk customers via SMS.

Impact

- ✓ **Churn rates reduced by 18%** with targeted retention strategies.
- ✓ **Increased customer loyalty** with personalized service recommendations.
- ✓ Enhanced **customer support efficiency** with AI-driven insights.

9. E-Commerce: AI-Powered Personalized Product Recommendations

Scenario
An online retailer wanted to **boost sales and customer engagement** by implementing **personalized product recommendations** based on browsing and purchasing history.

ANNEXURE D CASE STUDIES AND REAL-WORLD SCENARIOS

Fabric Solution:

- **Data Sources**
  - User browsing history and shopping cart data
  - Purchase history and return patterns
  - Customer reviews and ratings

- **Implementation**
  - **Streaming Dataflows** collected live shopping behavior from the website.
  - **Synapse Data Warehouse** stored structured customer transaction history.
  - AI-powered **recommendation algorithms** suggested products based on user preferences.
  - **KQL queries** analyzed buying trends and seasonal sales spikes.
  - **Power BI Dashboards** provided marketing teams with customer insights.
  - **Power Automate workflows** sent personalized discount offers via email.

Impact

- ✓ **Conversion rates increased by 22%** with AI-driven recommendations.
- ✓ **Customer engagement improved**, leading to higher retention.
- ✓ **Sales revenue grew** due to optimized cross-selling and upselling.

ANNEXURE D   CASE STUDIES AND REAL-WORLD SCENARIOS

10. Logistics: AI-Optimized Route Planning for Delivery Services

Scenario

A logistics company needed to **optimize delivery routes** to reduce transportation costs and improve **on-time deliveries**.

Fabric Solution:

- **Data Sources**
    - GPS tracking from delivery vehicles
    - Traffic and weather data
    - Customer delivery addresses and order volumes
- **Implementation**
    - **Real-time vehicle tracking data** was stored in **OneLake**.
    - AI-powered **route optimization algorithms** calculated the fastest delivery paths.
    - **KQL queries** analyzed live traffic data and adjusted routes dynamically.
    - **Power BI Dashboards** displayed delivery performance metrics.
    - **Automated alerts via Power Automate** notified drivers of roadblocks or delays.

Impact

- ✓ **Delivery efficiency improved by 30%** with AI-optimized routing.
- ✓ **Fuel costs reduced** by 20% due to optimized routes.
- ✓ **Customer satisfaction increased** with accurate delivery time predictions.

ANNEXURE E

DAX and Power Query Cheat Sheet

This annexure provides a quick reference guide for commonly used **DAX (Data Analysis Expressions)** and **Power Query M Language** functions. These tools are fundamental for data modeling, transformation, and reporting within Microsoft Fabric, especially in preparation for the DP-700 exam.

Section 1: DAX Cheat Sheet

DAX is used for defining calculations, aggregations, and expressions within semantic models. It is commonly applied in calculated columns, measures, and calculated tables.

ANNEXURE E   DAX AND POWER QUERY CHEAT SHEET

Commonly Used DAX Functions

Category	Function	Description/Example
Aggregation	SUM()	Calculates the total: SUM(Sales[Amount])
	AVERAGE()	Returns the mean value: AVERAGE(Employee[Salary])
	MAX(), MIN()	Returns the highest or lowest value in a column
	COUNT(), COUNTA()	Counts rows or non-blank entries
Logical	IF()	Returns a value based on a condition: IF([Profit] > 0, "Profit", "Loss")
	SWITCH()	Replaces multiple IF statements for better readability
	AND(), OR()	Combines multiple conditions
Filtering	CALCULATE()	Modifies the context of a calculation: CALCULATE(SUM(Sales[Amount]), Region[Name] = "East")
	FILTER()	Applies advanced filtering over a table
	ALL(), REMOVEFILTERS()	Removes filter context, used for percent-of-total or global aggregations
Time Intelligence	TOTALYTD()	Computes Year-to-Date values
	SAMEPERIODLASTYEAR()	Compares values across time periods
	DATESYTD(), DATEADD()	Shifts or aggregates data over time
Ranking	RANKX()	Ranks values in a table
Relationships	RELATED()	Accesses data from a related table
	USERELATIONSHIP()	Activates an inactive relationship for the calculation context

DAX Best Practices and Tips

1. **Use Measures over Calculated Columns**
   - Measures are evaluated at query time and are more memory-efficient.
   - Calculated columns are evaluated at data refresh and stored in memory, which may increase model size unnecessarily.

2. **Optimize with Variables (VAR)**
   - Declaring variables improves readability and performance by avoiding repeated evaluation.
   - Example:
     ```
     VAR TotalSales = SUM(Sales[Amount])
     RETURN IF(TotalSales > 100000,
     "High", "Low")
     ```

3. **Always Specify Filter Context with CALCULATE**
   - CALCULATE changes the context in which a measure is calculated and is the backbone of advanced DAX.
   - It can be used to apply filters dynamically based on slicer selections or user roles.

4. **Minimize Use of Row Context in Measures**
   - Measures operate in filter context; avoid using row context constructs like EARLIER() unless necessary.
   - Use iterators like SUMX() wisely for row-level calculations in aggregate measures.

ANNEXURE E   DAX AND POWER QUERY CHEAT SHEET

5. **Avoid Bi-Directional Relationships When Possible**

    - They can lead to ambiguous models and performance issues.

    - Prefer single-directional relationships and use CROSSFILTER() or USERELATIONSHIP() for specific calculations when needed.

6. **Test DAX Logic in Simple Models First**

    - For complex calculations, validate logic in a simplified model or with a subset of data.

7. **Use Built-in Time Intelligence with Proper Date Tables**

    - Ensure the date table is marked as a "Date Table" in the model.

    - Time functions require a continuous, complete date table with no gaps.

Section 2: Power Query (M Language) Cheat Sheet

Power Query is used in Microsoft Fabric for data preparation in Dataflows Gen2. The M language allows advanced data shaping, transformation, and cleaning.

ANNEXURE E DAX AND POWER QUERY CHEAT SHEET

Common Power Query Functions

Transformation	M Function/Syntax	Description/Example
Rename Columns	Table.RenameColumns(Source, {{"OldName", "NewName"}})	Renames specified column(s)
Filter Rows	Table.SelectRows(Source, each [Amount] > 1000)	Filters rows based on conditions
Add Columns	Table.AddColumn(Source, "NewCol", each [Sales] * 0.1)	Adds a calculated column
Remove Columns	Table.RemoveColumns(Source, {"ColA", "ColB"})	Removes specified columns
Group By	Table.Group(Source, {"Category"}, {{"Total", each List.Sum([Amount]), type number}})	Aggregates values based on grouping
Merge Queries	Table.NestedJoin(...)	Joins two tables
Append Queries	Table.Combine({Table1, Table2})	Stacks queries vertically
Change Data Types	Table.TransformColumnTypes(Source, {{"Date", type date}})	Sets column data types
Replace Values	Table.ReplaceValue(Source, "Old", "New", Replacer.ReplaceText, {"Column1"})	Replaces values in one or more columns

Power Query Best Practices and Tips

1. **Minimize Applied Steps**
   - Combine steps where possible to reduce overhead. For example, do not split filtering and renaming into separate steps unless necessary.

2. **Use Descriptive Step Names**
   - Rename each step (not just the default names like "Changed Type1") to reflect its purpose. This improves readability and maintainability.

3. **Use Native Query Folding**
   - Power Query attempts to push transformations back to the source system (query folding). Favor transformations that support folding for performance.

4. **Avoid Repeated Column Type Conversions**
   - Apply data type conversions once, ideally after all transformations are completed, to avoid redundant processing.

5. **Handle Nulls Explicitly**
   - Replace or filter out nulls where required to prevent errors in downstream analysis.

6. **Parameterize Queries for Reusability**
   - Create parameters for dynamic data sources (e.g., start date, file path) to make your queries reusable and scalable.

ANNEXURE E   DAX AND POWER QUERY CHEAT SHEET

7. **Test Query Performance on Sample Data**

    - During development, apply filters to reduce the dataset size and test transformations quickly.

8. **Use the Advanced Editor to Understand M Code**

    - Editing or reviewing the underlying M script is helpful for understanding complex steps and debugging.

Summary Table: When to Use DAX vs. Power Query

Task Description	Use DAX	Use Power Query
Create interactive measures or KPIs	✓	
Merge multiple data sources		✓
Apply business logic dynamically	✓	
Clean and format raw data		✓
Aggregate data before loading to model		✓
Perform row-level calculations at query time	✓	

Index

A

AAD, *see* Azure Active Directory (AAD)
Absolute words, 189
Abstraction layer, 125
Accuracy, 131
Accurate demand forecasting, 285
ADF, *see* Azure Data Factory (ADF)
Ad hoc queries, 40
ADLS, *see* Azure Data Lake Storage (ADLS)
ADLS Gen2, *see* Azure Data Lake Storage Gen2 (ADLS Gen2)
Adventure Works, 215, 216, 218, 219, 222–225, 227–229
Aggregation tables, 244, 245
Aggregations, 120, 136, 139, 141, 142, 257, 262
AI-driven insights, 50
AI-driven models, 283
AI-Powered Student Performance, 290, 291
All-in-one analytics platform, 33
Analytical assets, 4
Apache Kafka, 39
Audit logs, 183

Auto-discovery, 35
Automated restocking recommendations, 285
Automation, 62, 265
AutoML models, 39, 54, 285
Auto-optimization, 58
Auto-refreshing, 52
Auto-scaling, 32, 54
Average Revenue, 128
AWS S3, 58
Azure, 30, 34
Azure Active Directory (AAD), 64, 68, 82, 83
Azure Cognitive Services, 227
Azure Data Factory (ADF), 38, 64, 66, 82
Azure Data Gateway, 66
Azure Data Lake Storage (ADLS), 58
Azure Data Lake Storage Gen2 (ADLS Gen2), 65
Azure data security, 242
Azure DevOps, 257
Azure Event Hub, 66, 67
Azure Machine Learning, 284, 286
Azure ML integration, 38
Azure Monitor, 176
Azure services, 55, 202, 204

INDEX

Azure SQL Database, 35, 130, 132
Azure Synapse, 251
Azure Synapse Analytics, 78

B

Backup strategies, 169
Balance innovation, 270
BCP, *see* Business Continuity Planning (BCP)
Bi-directional relationships, 199, 300
Big data processing, 36
Binary decisions, 192
Blackouts, 291
Block Sharing, 166
Bonus, 276
Boost sales, 293
Built-in machine learning, 203
Built-in security, 53
Built on Delta Lake, 50
Bulk insert operations, 113
Business Continuity Planning (BCP), 170
Business intelligence workflows, 148
Business language, 274
Business logic, 126

C

Calculated columns, 139
Cardinality, 140
Central fact table, 255

Certification renewal
   Microsoft Fabric
      ecosystem, 21, 22
   preparation, 24
   process, 22, 23
   staying, 25
   updates, 23, 24
CI/CD, *see* Continuous Integration and Deployment (CI/CD)
Cloud Apps, 166
Cloud-based execution model, 32
CLS, *see* Column-level security (CLS)
Clustered Columnstore Indexes, 111
Clustered index, 111
CMK, *see* Customer-Managed Keys (CMK)
Co-Authoring, 147
Collaboration, 143, 147, 186, 247, 248, 269
Column-Level Encryption, 164
Column-level security (CLS), 9, 165
Columnstore index, 111
Common Table Expressions (CTEs), 245
Compliance, 178
Composite Mode, 200
Composite models, 244, 264
Compute nodes, 110
Consumption-based pricing model, 53
Continuous Integration and Deployment (CI/CD), 257

INDEX

Contoso Corporation, 214, 216–218, 220–223, 225–227, 229, 230
Copilot AI, 54, 62
Cost management, 261
Cost optimization, 64, 179
Credit card transactions, 286, 287
CTEs, *see* Common Table Expressions (CTEs)
Customer engagement, 293
Customer-Managed Keys (CMK), 164

D

Data access control, 243
Data Analysis Expressions (DAX), 3, 4, 25, 120, 128, 130, 245, 297
   built-in time intelligence, 300
   measures and calculations, 134, 135
   storage mode, 140, 141
   simple models, 300
   cheat sheet, 297, 298
   query performance, 139, 140
Data analytics and platforms, 269
Database level, 97
Data cataloging tools, 147
Data classification
   capabilities, 182
   importance of, 181
   policy enforcement, 184, 185
Data-driven organizations, 2

Data-driven strategy, 292
Data encryption, 243
Data engineering, 59, 78, 251
   and ETL, 66
Data Fabric, 248
Data Factory, 31, 37, 38, 46, 52, 93, 251, 252, 262
Data Factory pipelines, 35, 45, 194
Dataflows, 93, 112, 133, 241, 252, 253
Dataflows Gen2, 35, 300
Data governance, 178, 179, 247, 264
   and security, 55
Data ingestion, 241
Data integration, 59, 60
Data integrity, 90, 92
Data lake, 248
Data life cycle, 44–46
   interoperable workflows, 45
   Microsoft Purview, 46
   storage, 45
   unified data lake, 44–46
Data lineage, 182, 183, 247
Data lineage tracking, 58
Data loss prevention (DLP), 151, 162, 166, 182, 184
Data management, 110
Data masking, 242
Data model documentation, 143
Data modeling, 264, 280
Data modelling concepts
   certification, 85
   data normalization *vs.* denormalization, 89, 90
   data storage options, 85, 86

307

INDEX

Data modelling concepts (*cont.*)
    fact and dimension tables, 88, 89
    Microsoft Fabric, 85
    performance
        optimization, 91, 92
    relationships & indexing, 90–92
    snowflake schema, 87, 88
    star Schema *vs.* snowflake
        schema, 86, 87
Data model structure, 138
Data Pipelines, 3, 31, 93, 94, 253, 281
    ETL, 105
Data preparation, 12
    data Pipelines, 241
    data wrangling *vs.* data
        cleaning, 241
    and ETL, 252
    querying and analytical
        techniques, 14, 15
    transformation, 241
    transformation
        techniques, 13–15
Data processing, 31
Data quality, 145, 146, 178, 186
Data quality issues, 3
Data Refresh, 175, 176
Data refresh scheduling, 120
Data retention, 170, 243
Data Science, 59, 251, 260
Data security, 185, 253
    and compliance, 151, 162–170
Data sensitivity, 242
Data storage, 173
    monitoring tools, 114
    partitioning and
        distribution, 108–111
    performance, 107
    query performance tuning,
        113, 114
Data tokenization, 164
Data transformation techniques,
    36, 241, 252
Data warehouse, 31, 59, 78, 86, 95,
    130, 133, 215, 240, 248, 251
    configuring, 82
    creation, 81
    data modeling concepts, 73
    key features, 79
    metrics, 114
    Microsoft Fabric, 78
    practice tests, 193
    setting up, 80, 81
    sources connection, 82
    storage, 107–114
Data wrangling, 241
DAX query shortcuts, 280
DDM, *see* Dynamic Data
    Masking (DDM)
Decision-making processes, 2
Delta Lake, 242
    compatibility, 35
    format, 104
Delta Lake Time Travel, 197
Delta Tables, 194
Denormalization, 89, 90
Deployment, 265
Deployment pipelines, 10, 144
Descriptive attributes, 95

INDEX

Design principles, 131
Detailed interview, 275–277
Dimension tables, 86, 87, 89, 95, 133, 255
Direct filtering, 142
Direct Lake access, 45
Direct Lake Mode, 34, 104, 105
DirectQuery Mode, 243, 244
Disaster recovery (DR), 169
Documentation, 143, 147
DP-600
    Microsoft Fabric Analytics Engineer Associate, 107
DP-600 certification, 17, 93, 187
DP-600 Exam Preparation, 26–28
DP-600: Microsoft Fabric Analytics Engineer Associate exam, 188
Drill-down analysis, 135
Drill-down functionality, 129
DR, *see* Disaster recovery (DR)
DR planning, 177
Dynamic calculations, 135
Dynamic Data Masking (DDM), 164
Dynamic groups, 158

E

E-Commerce, 47, 293, 294
Education, 290, 291
EHR, *see* Electronic Health Records (EHR)
Electronic Health Records (EHR), 283
ELT, *see* Extract, Load, Transform (ELT)
Encryption, 68, 163, 164, 253
Endorsement, 9
Enterprise-grade security and governance, 61
Entra ID groups, 181
ETL, *see* Extract, Transform, Load (ETL)
Event-driven analytics, 39
Event-driven ETL, 105
Eventstream, 265
Evolution of data analytics, 29
Exam preparation strategies
    exam day strategies, 237, 238
    hands-on practice, 236
    mock exams, 237
    objectives, 235
    official and reliable resources, 236
    post-exam learning, 238
    study groups and communities, 237
    time management, 236
Extract, Load, Transform (ELT), 31, 93, 241
    Data Factory Pipelines, 94
    data pipelines, 105
    data sources connection, 93
    Direct Lake Mode, 105, 106
    in Microsoft Fabric, 106, 107
    security & governance, 106
    transformation, 94, 95
Extract, Transform, Load (ETL), 31, 37, 74, 93, 112, 241

INDEX

F

Fabric administration, 263
Fabric Analytics Engineer, 269
Fabric architecture, 262
Fabric Capacity Metrics App, 173
Fabric Direct Lake mode, 87
Fabric projects, 267
Fabric report, 266, 268
Fabric tool, 267
Fabric workloads, 259, 260
Fabrikam Inc., 215–217, 219–222, 224–226, 228, 230
Fact tables, 86, 88, 89, 133, 142, 244, 255
FK, *see* Foreign keys (FK)
Foreign keys (FK), 90, 134
Fraud cases, 286
Fraud detection, 286, 287

G

Geo-Redundant Storage (GRS), 169
GitHub Actions, 257
Google Cloud, 69
Governance, 143
  best practices, 152
  framework, 179, 180
  improvement, 184, 185
Govern Microsoft Fabric
  authentication methods, 156
  logging and auditing, 169
  user and access management, 155–163
GRS, *see* Geo-Redundant Storage (GRS)

H

Hands-on workshops, 274
Hash distribution, 111
Hash partitioning, 109
Healthcare, 283, 284
Hierarchies, 135
High customer churn rates, 292
High-pressure project, 270
High-quality data analysis, 148
High-risk patients, 283
Hybrid Mode, 244

I, J

IAM, *see* Identity and Access Management (IAM)
Identity and Access Management (IAM), 163
Identify at-risk students, 290
Import mode, 244
Incremental loads, 104
Indexing, 107, 120
Indexing strategies, 90, 91
Individual users, 158
Industry-specific, 167
Infrastructure costs, 54
Interactive dashboards, 40

INDEX

Interview questions and
  answers, 251–270
IoT Hub, 67, 68
Item-level access controls, 8

K

Key best practices, 131
Key performance indicators
  (KPIs), 4, 273
KQL databases, 286
KPIs, *see* Key performance
  indicators (KPIs)
KQL, *see* Kusto Query
  Language (KQL)
Kusto Query Language (KQL), 3, 4,
  15, 25, 31, 52, 66, 176,
  245, 281

L

Lakehouse, 31, 79, 80, 82, 86, 93,
  104, 108, 115, 130, 133,
  240, 285
Lakehouse data, 67
Learning curve, 272
Learning management system
  (LMS), 290
Learning plan, 271
Life cycle management, 143, 147, 148
Line Chart, 201
List partitioning, 109
Litware Inc., 215, 217–219, 221, 222,
  224, 226, 227, 230

Live practice, 274
LMS, *see* Learning management
  system (LMS)
Logistics, 295, 296
Log management, 175, 176
Long scenario, 190
Low-code Dataflows, 45
Low-code Dataflows Gen2, 37

M

Machine learning (ML), 260
  integration, 67, 68
  models, 38
Manage time, 191
Match items, 189
Medallion Architecture, 242, 252
MFA, *see* Multi-factor
  authentication (MFA)
Microsoft 365 (Excel, Teams,
  SharePoint), 34, 54
Microsoft documentation, 271
Microsoft Entra ID groups, 151,
  155, 156, 158, 180
Microsoft Fabric, 30, 73, 78, 92, 119,
  133, 142, 162–170, 187, 219,
  222, 239, 241, 251, 259, 266
  AI-powered insights, 54
  architecture
    business intelligence, 61
    core components, 57
    data analytics, 56
    data integration, 59, 60
    lake-centric approach, 56

INDEX

Microsoft Fabric (*cont.*)
    OneLake, 58
    real-time analytics, 60, 61
    scalability &
      performance, 62, 63
    security, compliance and
      governance, 61, 62
    Synapse Analytics, 59
  automating performance
    optimization, 177
    self-healing, 177
  availability and disaster
    recovery, 176, 177
  business use cases
    financial services, 48
    healthcare & and life
      sciences, 48
    manufacturing, 48
    retail and
      E-commerce, 47, 48
  centralized and scalable
    approach, 33
  core capabilities, 34–43
  cost efficiency, 54
  data life cycle, 44–46
  data modelling concepts, 85–92
  data platforms, 49
  data refresh performance,
    174, 175
  definition, 33
  ETL process, 92–107
  governance, 178
  key features, 49
    AI-Powered Insights, 50
    built-in security, 53
    consumption-based pricing
      model, 53
    data factory, 52
    real-time analytics, 51
    Synapse, 51
    unified data and
      analytics, 50, 51
  loading data, 104
  logging and auditing, 175, 176
  monitoring tools, 170, 171
  multiple tools, 33
  predictive analytics, 38
  queries optimization, 172
    data pipelines, 172, 173
    indexing, 172
    resource and capacity
      management, 173, 174
  same portal, 46
  scalability, 34
  scalability and performance, 55
  simplicity and ease of use, 53
  third-party tools, 55, 68, 69
  vs. traditional data analytics, 47
  unified data repository, 54
  use cases, 41–44
  See also Data warehouse
Microsoft Fabric Analytics
    Engineer
  data preparation, 11–15
  multinational retail, 285, 286
  responsibilities, 2–4
  role-based responsibilities, 7, 8
  semantic models, 15–17

skills (*see* Skill domain)
stakeholders and collaborations, 5-8
understanding and analytical thinking, 271-275
Microsoft Fabric Analytics Engineers, 251, 275-277
Microsoft Fabric Compliance Certifications, 167
Microsoft Fabric Data Pipelines, 285
Microsoft Fabric Shortcuts, 279
Microsoft Purview, 34, 46, 53, 58, 61, 64, 78, 147, 168, 185, 243, 253
  with Azure, 68
ML, *see* Machine learning (ML)
Model creation process, 131
Model governance, 143
Model life cycle, 148
Model management
  data quality and consistency, 145, 146
  documentation and collaboration, 147
  life cycle management, 147, 148
  optimization, 146, 147
  security and access control, 145
  structured model governance strategy, 143, 144
  version control, 144
Monitoring and performance optimization, 151
Multi-Cloud Compatibility, 32

Multi-factor authentication (MFA), 53, 62, 152, 155, 162, 181, 185
Multi-layered security model, 163
Multiple correct answers, 189
Multiple questions, 190

N

Naming Convention, 144
Naming pattern, 143
Natural language, 51
Non-clustered index, 111
Non-technical stakeholder, 267
Normalization, 89, 90
Notebooks, 93, 112, 260, 282

O

OAuth and OpenID Connect (OIDC), 156
Object-level security (OLS), 129, 136, 145, 166
OLS, *see* Object-level security (OLS)
OIDC, *see* OAuth and OpenID Connect (OIDC)
One correct answer, 188
OneDrive, 147
OneLake, 12, 30, 34, 37, 82, 108, 130, 239, 248, 251, 282, 283, 285, 291
  analytics workloads, 35
  data sources, 35

INDEX

OneLake (*cont.*)
    Direct Lake mode, 36
    integration with Azure
        data, 65, 66
    key features
        centralized data
            storage, 50
        shortcuts feature, 50
    multiple systems, 35
    tables, 132
One-to-many (1:M), 134, 199
One-to-one (1:1), 134
On-time deliveries, 295
Operational efficiency, 179, 186
Optimize delivery routes, 295
Optimize electricity
    distribution, 291
Out-of-stock issues, 285

P

PAM, *see* Privileged Access
    Management (PAM)
Parallel query execution, 110
Parquet, 194
Partitioning, 120
Partition pruning, 113
Pay-as-you-go model, 54
PBAC, *see* Policy-based access
    control (PBAC)
Performance, 131
Performance degradation, 143
Performance optimization
    techniques, 85, 257

Personalized product
    recommendations, 293
PIM, *see* Privileged Identity
    Management (PIM)
PK, *see* Primary keys (PK)
POCs, *see* Proof of
    Concepts (POCs)
Point of Sale (POS), 285
Policy-based access control
    (PBAC), 152, 181, 185
PoLP, *see* Principle of least
    privilege (PoLP)
POS, *see* Point of Sale (POS)
Power Automate, 284
Power Automate notifications, 290
Power BI, 32–34, 45, 46, 56, 61, 69,
    78, 130, 133, 136, 138, 198,
    200, 243, 251, 252, 256, 259,
    261, 266, 273, 280, 283, 284,
    287, 290, 292–294
    Copilot, 40
    embedded in Microsoft
        Fabric, 40
    integration, 52
Power BI Dashboard, 285
Power Query, 302, 303
Power query (M language), 300–303
Practice tests
    data warehousing, 193–197
    drag and drop, 189, 190
    exam preparation strategies, 188
    multiple choice questions,
        188, 189
    question types

dropdown questions, 192
hotspot, 192, 193
scenario-based
 questions, 191
question types breakdown
 case studies, 190, 191
semantic models, 197–201
technical knowledge, 188
Precomputed aggregates, 91
Predictive analytics, 283, 284
Predictive models, 290
Primary keys (PK), 90, 134
Principle of least privilege (PoLP), 162, 180
Privileged Access Management (PAM), 243
Privileged Identity Management (PIM), 158
Process-of-elimination, 189
Proof of Concepts (POCs), 270
Python/ML Shortcuts, 282

Q

Query Execution Plans, 114
Query optimization techniques, 107, 120
Query speed, 91

R

Range Partitioning, 77, 109, 116
RBAC, *see* Role-based access control (RBAC)

Real-time analytics, 31, 33, 39, 40, 51, 59–61, 66, 191, 218, 248, 249, 251, 256
 Azure, 66, 67
Real-time anomaly detection, 52
Real-time dashboards, 54, 223
Real-time data ingestion, 105
Real-time data streaming analytics, 204
Real-Time Hub, 12
Real-time monitoring, 45
Real-time risk scores, 284
Real-time traffic flow data, 288
Real-World Benefit, 46
Real-world business problem, 191
Replicated tables, 111
Requirements and constraints, 190
Resource-intensive, 139
Responsiveness, 138
Retail, 285, 286
Revamped Data Factory, 52
 in Fabric, 38
RLS, *see* Row-level security (RLS)
Role-based access control (RBAC), 32, 53, 62, 68, 83, 120, 126, 136, 137, 151, 152, 156, 165, 178, 185
 implementation, 180
Round-robin, 111
Row-by-row computations, 139
Row context, 299

INDEX

Row-level security (RLS), 9, 84, 92, 106, 126, 129, 136, 137, 145, 152, 165, 181, 200, 253
    filtering, 142, 143
Running list, 272

S

SalesData, 87
SAP on-premises, 66
Scalability, 131, 138
Scaling, 174
SCDs, *see* Slowly changing dimensions (SCDs)
Scenario-based critical thinking, 266, 267
Scenario-based questions, 257, 258
Seamlessly transition, 50
Security, 4, 143, 186
    filters, 120
    and governance, 32, 33
    and maintenance, 242, 243
    monitoring, 168
    vulnerabilities, 143
Self-healing, 177
Self-service analytics, 126, 247
Semantic models, 4, 119, 215
    abstraction layer, 125
    business-friendly representation, 125
    business understanding, 132
    data access, 126
    data analysis expressions, 134, 135
    data analytics solution, 17, 18
    data preparation, 18, 19
    data refresh, 135
    designing, 136, 137
    designing and building, 15, 16
    enterprise-scale, 16, 17
    implementation and management, 19, 20
    implementing and managing, 243–245
    in Microsoft Fabric, 119, 126, 130–133
    model management, 143–148
    optimization
        data model design, 138
        data refresh performance, 141
        datasets, 137
        in Microsoft Fabric, 137
        performance, 137
        query performance, 139, 140
        security and role-level filtering, 142, 143
    performance, 126
    performance tuning, 120
    practices in managing, 120
    practice tests, 197–201
    question set, 202–235
    real-world use cases, 131
    relationships, 128
    sales data model structure, 133
    storage mode, 130, 135
    tables and columns, 126
    tables and data structure, 133

user-friendly analytics, 119
weightage, 20
Sensitivity, 181, 182
Sensitivity labels, 9, 166, 167
Sentiment analysis, 293
Separate tools, 50
Shared and reused data, 50
Shared compute engine, 44
SharePoint, 147
Simple one-page guides, 274
Single Direction Filtering, 134
Single-direction relationships, 138
Single SaaS environment, 44
Single Sign-On (SSO), 68, 155
Skill domain
    development life cycle of analytics, 9–11
    life cycle management practices, 8
    security and governance, 8, 9
Slowly changing dimensions (SCDs) 95–103, 197
    SCD Type 0, 97
    SCD Type 1, 97, 98
    SCD Type 2, 98, 99
    SCD Type 3, 99
    SCD Type 4, 100
    SCD Type 6, 101
Smart city traffic optimization, 288, 289
Smart grid-energy consumption optimization, 291, 292
Snowflake schema, 86–88, 133, 138, 245

Soft Skills, 276
Source control repositories, 144
Spark jobs, 112
Spark Notebooks, 95
Specific access levels, 158
Speed, 138
Speeds up queries, 110
SQL, *see* Structured Query Language (SQL)
SQL Databases, 83
SQL Joins, 246
SQL queries, 83, 255, 256
SQL Query Editor Shortcuts, 281
SSO, *see* Single Sign-On (SSO)
Stakeholder
    business, 5
    collaboration, 5–8, 247, 248
Star schema, 86, 87, 92, 133, 136, 138, 142, 245, 255
STAR technique, 275
Stock shortages and overstocking, 285
Storage optimization, 84
Streaming dataflows, 294
Structured data, 108
Structured format, 104
Structured Query Language (SQL), 3, 245
Synapse Analytics, 130, 132
Synapse Data Engineering, 36, 37, 51
Synapse Data Science, 38, 45, 51
    in Fabric, 38, 39
Synapse Data Warehouses, 283, 284, 290, 294

INDEX

Synapse Notebooks, 46
Synapse-powered analytics, 56
Synapse Real-Time Analytics, 39, 45
Synapse Spark notebooks, 45

T

Table distribution, 110
Technical challenges, 268
Telecom, 292, 293
Test-taking strategies, 188
Threat detection, 168
Three-tier environment, 148
Timestamps, 140
Total Sales, 128
Traffic congestion and pollution, 288
Transaction-level data, 141
Transformation techniques, 141
  aggregation & preprocessing, 103
  data, 13–15
  data cleansing & standardization, 95
Troubleshooting, 261
T-SQL (Transact-SQL), 115

U

Unified data platform, 78
Unified storage layer, 115
Unused access, 161
User access, 161
User and Access Management, 151
User-friendly interface, 53
User roles, 180, 181

V

Variables (VAR), 299
Version control, 143, 144
Version control systems, 10
Version tracking, 148
Visual relationship modeling, 134

W

Watermark Columns, 104
Weightage, 20, 21
WHERE Clauses, 113
Window Functions, 246
Workspace-level access controls, 8
Workspace Permissions, 136

X, Y, Z

XMLA endpoints, 11

GPSR Compliance

The European Union's (EU) General Product Safety Regulation (GPSR) is a set of rules that requires consumer products to be safe and our obligations to ensure this.

If you have any concerns about our products, you can contact us on

ProductSafety@springernature.com

In case Publisher is established outside the EU, the EU authorized representative is:

Springer Nature Customer Service Center GmbH
Europaplatz 3
69115 Heidelberg, Germany

www.ingramcontent.com/pod-product-compliance
Lightning Source LLC
LaVergne TN
LVHW010336260326
834688LV00036B/734